THE PATH OF DUTY

TO

*The one who gains freedom
by granting it to others.*

LEONARD E. READ

THE PATH OF DUTY

The Foundation for Economic Education, Inc.
Irvington-on-Hudson, New York 10533
1982

THE AUTHOR AND PUBLISHER

Leonard E. Read has been president of The Foundation for Economic Education since it was organized in 1946.

The Foundation is a nonpolitical, nonprofit, educational institution. Its senior staff and numerous writers are students as well as teachers of the free market, private ownership, limited government rationale. Sample copies of the Foundation's monthly study journal, *The Freeman,* are available on request.

Published September 1982

ISBN-0-910614-69-5

CONTENTS

1

THE PATH OF DUTY

If you have no friends to share or rejoice in your success in life—if you cannot look back to those to whom you owe gratitude, or forward to those to whom you ought to afford protection, still it is no less incumbent on you to move steadily in the path of duty; for your active exertions are due not only to society; but in humble gratitude to the Being who made you a member of it, with powers to serve yourself and others.

—WALTER SCOTT

Sir Walter Scott (1772–1832), Scottish novelist and poet, pronounced more clearly than anyone known to me, the numerous attributes which, if understood and adhered to, would assure the freedom way of life. He gave us the intellectual and spiritual formula for doing one's duty. The following are supporting observations and commentaries on commendable actions.

"Our grand business," wrote Thomas Carlyle, "is not to see what lies dimly at a distance, but to do what lies clearly at hand." Thus did he warn us against vainly trying to foretell the future.

So, let us do what lies clearly at hand—right now! This is the formula for structuring a joyous and rewarding future. Let us, as Scott suggested, live in humble gratitude to the Creator of this marvelous universe. Our duty is to advance the freedom way of life, thereby serving ourselves and others.

From the American theologian Theodore Parker (1810–1860) comes this powerful urge to duty: "Let us do our duty in our shop or our kitchen; in the market, in the street, in office, the school, the home, just as faithfully as if we were in the front rank of some great battle and knew that victory for mankind depended on our bravery, strength and skill. When we do that, the humblest of us will be serving in that great army which achieves the welfare of the world."

As a guide to duty, it would be difficult to improve upon the Ten Commandments:

Fear God and keep his commandments; for this is the whole duty of man.
You shall not make unto thee any graven image.
You shall not take the name of the Lord your God in vain.
Observe the Sabbath day and keep it holy.
Honor your father and your mother.
You shall not kill.
You shall not commit adultery.
You shall not steal.
You shall not give false testimony against your neighbor.
You shall not covet.

Emerson stressed the importance of self-responsibility: "What I must do is all that concerns me, not what the people think."

This importance of self-responsibility also was stressed

by William Ernest Hocking, Harvard professor of philosophy:

> For in the last analysis, the thought and conscience of the individual man are the only thought and conscience there are. . . . There is, in literal truth, no public mind; there are only the minds of the persons composing the public. There is no public conscience; there are only their several consciences. Dry these functions up, or bind the life out of them, and all the mental and moral life of the public is stopped at its source.

The English poet, Aubrey De Vere (1788–1846), adds this: "This span of life was lent for lofty duties, not for selfishness, not to be whiled away in aimless dreams but to improve ourselves and serve mankind."

I fully endorse De Vere's concluding thought and commend self-improvement as the only way to serve mankind.

Not everyone, however, is willing to work at self-improvement. There is a powerful temptation to improve others. It was against that temptation that we were warned by the English clergyman Thomas Fuller (1608–61): "Thou must content thyself to see the world as it is. Thou wilt never have any quiet if thou vexest thyself because thou canst not bring mankind to that exact notion of things and rule of life which thou has formed in thy own mind!"

Goethe also shared Fuller's point of view: "Man is not here to solve the problems of the universe, but to find out what he has to do and to restrain himself within the limits of his comprehension."

The English educator Thomas Arnold (1795–1842) added this good advice: "Use your gifts faithfully, and they shall be enlarged; practice what you know, and you shall attain to higher knowledge."

The relatively few citizens who believe in the freedom way of life fall into two categories: (1) the pessimists who see no end to the growing socialism—doomsday in the offing; and (2) the optimists who have faith in the recovery of freedom.

To repeat what I have written many times: All history attests to the fact that devolution—the decline into socialism—is, with few exceptions, followed by evolution, with progress inching ahead over the millennia. This is why I feel certain that a turnabout—liberty for one and all—is to bless our nation once again!

Thomas Fuller, on another occasion, had this thought: "The world is a Ladder for some to go up, and others down." Envision a ladder infinite in its tallness. Most people, if on the second step, look down with disdain at those on the first. Unless the person on any step looks up to those on the higher rungs, he will experience regress and not progress. That person will go down intellectually.

On the other hand, there are a few on the second step who, by reason of their high aspirations and accomplishments, cause those on the first step to seek their tutorship. But, equally important, they look to those on the above steps, learning from them. The more they ascend, the more mankind is graced with exemplars.

Let me conclude by quoting, as I often do, from the Father of our country, George Washington: "The consideration that human happiness and moral duty are inseparably connected, will always continue to prompt me to promote the former by inculcating the latter." Thus does doing one's duty lead to happiness and freedom.

2

THE PURPOSE OF WEALTH

The way to wealth is as plain as the way to market. It depends chiefly on two words, industry and frugality; that is, waste neither time nor money, but make the best use of both. Without industry and frugality, nothing will do; and with them everything.
—BENJAMIN FRANKLIN

As related to monetary wealth, Franklin's formula is doubtless correct. Assume its attainment. Does it enrich the attainers? The answer, in my view, is "No," if the wealth results in early retirement—life's highest mission abandoned. The answer is "Yes," if attainment results in an awareness of life's greatest wealth—an awareness, perception, consciousness of the freedom philosophy and how better to explain it. Briefly, advance to the point that others will seek one's tutorship.

Ever so many of our citizens think of wealth as a gigantic accumulation of dollars. To them millionaires exemplify the wealthy. They would envy a late friend of mine who was a billionaire. True, the more dollars one possesses the wealthier one is in a materialistic sense. This, however, is far from wealth in its most laudable sense. Wrote Henry Ward Beecher, the American clergyman (1813–87): "No man can tell whether he is rich or poor by turning to his ledger. It is the heart that makes a man rich. He is rich according to what he is, not according to what he has."

The heart in this sense refers to courage, dauntlessness, resolution, and spirit. Dollars may aid this worthy goal but it is the celestial attainment that matters!

The Arabian religious teacher and founder of Mohammedanism, Mahomet (570–630), offered these guidelines: "When a man dies, the people ask, 'What has he left behind him?' But the angels, as they bend over his grave, inquire, 'What good deeds has thou sent on before thee?' "

As to good deeds, ponder these thoughts:

The American clergyman George D. Boardman (1828–1903): "Our deeds are seeds of fate, sown here on earth, but bringing forth their harvest in eternity."

The American poet Henry Wadsworth Longfellow (1807–82): "Our deeds follow us, and what we have been makes us what we are."

The English dramatist Richard Sheridan (1751–1816): "A life spent worthily should be measured by deeds not years."

The Spanish dramatist, poet and novelist, Cervantes (1547–1616): "Good actions ennoble us, and we are the sons of our deeds."

Good deeds are, indeed, good answers to what the angels ask!

What a variation in the assessment of wealth by sages past and present, ranging all the way from commendation to condemnation! There is a good reason for these differing evaluations: wealth has good effects on some people, bad effects on others. Here is one of the many derogatory statements about wealth:

> Can wealth give happiness?
> Look 'round and see—
> What gay distress!
> What splendid misery!
> Whatever fortune lavishly can pour,
> The mind annihilates, and calls for
> more.   *—Oliver Goldsmith*

Let me share a personal experience that is not derogatory but joyful. My annual salary when General Manager of the Los Angeles Chamber of Commerce in the early forties was $18,000. One day the head of the country's largest insurance company offered me the job of heading their affairs in the seven western states. Said he, "Leonard, I do not know how much you will earn but I guarantee it will not be less than $100,000." I replied, "No, thank you."

Later I turned down two other offers. One was the Presidency of the National Association of Manufacturers; the other, Executive Vice President of the International Chamber of Commerce, headquarters in Paris. In each case the salaries were comparable to the previous offer.

Why these turndowns? They were not my cup of tea, as the British say. Mine? Working to improve an understanding of and a desire for the freedom way of life! A billion dollars would not swerve me from this aim any more than would ten cents! To me, my work is joyful, and joyfulness is a wonderful attribute, a blessing!

Another turndown. Three years ago FEE's Board of Trustees voted to raise my salary by $20,000. I refused this generous act. Why? I am already wealthy! I enjoy countless blessings in return for the little I do—writing and sharing freedom ideas and ideals with those who are interested in our philosophy.

The thousands of financial supporters of FEE over the past thirty-five years have made it possible for me to lecture and discuss our way of life in 48 of our states, time and again, and in 22 foreign nations. They made it possible for me to purchase this remarkable home for FEE, built in 1889. I couldn't dream of a more perfect workshop. And I am richly blest with my staff associates and 40 Trustees more pure in the freedom philosophy than any other Board known to me.

There are thousands of persons in America whose assets exceed a million dollars. There are billionaires, and possibly a few trillionaires. Some of this wealth is self-made, but it is inflation that has created the other millionaires and billionaires. In Germany, for instance, when the inflation reached the point that thirty million marks wouldn't buy a loaf of bread, trillionaires were a dime a dozen.

These observations lead me to the conclusion that adding up dollar assets is not necessarily the best way to decide who is rich and who is not. Actually, this is the old-world way of assessing wealth: acres of land, size of castle, number and quantity of jewels, how many serfs, slaves, servants or ducats in the vault. On this basis the legendary Midas, Croesus, kings of England, and German trillionaires would be accounted richer than I am. *And I say they are not!*

Who, in my view, are the wealthy in its highest sense? Those who believe in and strive for that high ideal of liberty.

3

HOW TO BECOME A MILLIONAIRE

*There are so many ways you can be-
come a millionaire in creative living.
It is a matter of a lifetime search for
ideas, words, sights, sounds, feelings, ideals, habits, and experiences
that will make your life an adventure
in growth.*
—WILFERD A. PETERSON

For years Mr. Peterson has written a brilliant article each
month in *Science of Mind* magazine.

I was so intrigued with his article entitled "How To Become a Millionaire" in the February 1982 issue that I asked
and received his permission to use it, along with a few
commentaries of my own.

This friend and I see eye to eye on ever so many subjects.
Creative living should be our number one aspiration, that is,
striving to approximate as nearly as possible the will of
God—Creation! He enumerates the ideas, ideals and other
objectives for which we should search. They exist by the
millions, indeed, by the billions!

9

Searching for these objectives, he suggests, will make our lives an adventure in growth, that is, striving for maturity, as noble an objective as one can have! Strive day in and day out for a growth in awareness, perception, consciousness. It is the growth of consciousness in our earthly lives that prescribes what we shall be in the Hereafter. As the English poet Lord Byron (1788–1824) wrote: "Man's conscience is the oracle of God."

You can become a millionaire by thinking a million great thoughts. In my book, *Let Freedom Reign,* there is a chapter entitled, "Confessions of a Rich Man," in which I acknowledged the source of some of my possessions:

Applying concepts conceived during the past six or seven generations, I may be among the very rich. And bear in mind that I do not have many dollars stashed away.

First, consider the little I do—not a single thing which, by itself, sustains life. I only read, write and lecture on behalf of the freedom way of life, a theoretician of sorts. Now, observe the goods and services I obtain in exchange for the infinitesimal mite I offer on the market. It would take a long book to list what I receive from others in exchange for what I do. Let a few examples suffice. Others make my pens and pencils, typewriter, airplanes, telephones that send my voice around the earth in one-seventh of a second. No one knows how to make such a simple thing as a pencil. A 747 jet has 5,000,000 parts and no person—past or present—knows how to make a single one of them!

I could not expect to survive if I had to live on only that which I now produce, a mere trifle. Compared to the millions of individuals and the countless variations in their occupations, I approximate zero. Nevertheless, "My cup runneth over." I "cast my bread upon the water" and what I receive in return for the little I do makes me a millionaire many times over.

Here is another way the two of us record experiences: each of us keeps a journal. I have kept mine for nearly thirty years, never missing a day. It begins in the morning with a prayer: "God, may my love for Thee motivate my actions and my thoughts for this day." My records are completed each day.

I write these in long-hand, have them typed by my secretary, and at the end of each year put them into bound volumes. There are now fifty volumes and approximately 2,500,000 words. The beginning? One evening in Texas I wrote a lecture I had promised to deliver to a church in Los Angeles two months later. The ideas came to me as if by magic, an experience so unusual and rewarding that I then and there resolved to keep a journal. The first two months were laborious, tiresome. I was tempted to call it quits. However, resolutions are made to be kept, not abandoned. And then the reward: it became one of the greatest joys of my life. That Peterson and Read are millionaires is an understatement!

Enjoyment is not the only reason for keeping a daily journal. Ideas, insights, foresights, intuitive flashes, if not recorded on reception, are like dreams, ephemeral, fleeting, gone with the wind. Countless individuals are far more brilliant than the few of us who keep journals. Were they to adopt this discipline? Supermen, graced with an extraordinary power of creativity! Achievement of freedom for one and all is not a numbers problem. So, let us hope that one or two more will either begin to keep a journal, or else immediately record on reception the thoughts that flash into their minds.

My millionaire companion suggests that one fill the pages of his journal with love, joy, courage, faith, forgiveness, peace and happiness. It is interesting to note what several great thinkers have had to say about these virtues.

Goethe: "We are shaped and fashioned by what we love."

Shakespeare: "Love looks not with the eye, but with the mind."

David H. Lawrence: "Love is a thing to be learned. It is difficult, complex maintenance of individual integrity throughout the incalculable processes of human polarity."

Robert South: "The very society of joy redoubles it; so that, while it lights on my friend it rebounds upon myself, and the brighter his candle burns, the more easily will it light mine."

Richard Sibbes: "We can do nothing well without joy, and a good conscience which is the ground of joy."

Paul Whitehead: "True courage is not the brutal force of vulgar heroes, but the firm resolve of virtue and reason."

Confucius: "To see what is right and not do it is the want of courage."

Francis Bacon: "There was never found in any age of the world, either philosopher or sect, or law, or discipline which did so highly exalt the public good as the Christian faith."

E. G. Bulwer-Lytton: "Strike from mankind the principle of faith, and men would have no more history than a flock of sheep."

Alexander Pope: "To err is human; to forgive divine."

Edward Thompson: "Peace is the happy, natural state of man; war, his corruption, his disgrace."

Edmund Spenser: "Lovely concord and most sacred peace doth nourish virtue, and fast friendship breed."

Emerson: "Nothing can bring you peace but yourself; nothing can bring you peace but the triumph of principles."

Philip G. Hamerton: "The happiest life is that which constantly exercises and educates which is best in us."

Samuel T. Coleridge: "Happiness can be built only on virtue, and must of necessity have truth for its foundation."

The above are samplings of the many sages Peterson and Read drew upon, making our lives, as he phrases it, "an adventure in growth." A person who has nothing more than a million dollars is, indeed, poor.

Hail to those who have become aware of the millions times millions of the tiny bits of individual expertise which, when free to flow, configurate and assure the freedom way of life for one and all.

> But whoso looketh into the perfect law of Liberty, and continueth therein, he being not a forgetful hearer, but a doer of the work, this man shall be blessed in his deed.
>
> —*James* 1:25

4

VANITY AND VIRTUE

Oh Vanity, how little is thy force acknowledged, or thy operations discerned! How wantonly dost thou deceive mankind, under different disguises! Sometimes thou dost wear the face of pity; sometimes of generosity; nay, thou hast the assurance to put on those glorious ornaments which belong only to heroic virtue.
—HENRY FIELDING

This English novelist (1707–54) clearly perceived the distinction between two opposites: Vanity and Virtue. Vanity is defined as ''self-admiration, self-conceit, self-love.'' Without question, this vainglory accounts for the growing socialism that presently bedevils all nations, the U.S.A. no exception.

As to vanity, *how little is thy force acknowledged, or thy operations discerned!* Accomplished devotees of freedom are the few who discern this self-conceitedness, and few they are. Relative to the several billions who inhabit this earth, their number is a tiny fraction.

How wantonly dost thou deceive mankind, under different

14

disguises. The victims of vanity are pretenders in ever so many ways. Politicians pretend to look after the poor, for instance, with food stamps, to cite one of many examples, and to guarantee their future with social security. These two interventions are but a fraction of their nonsense. Result? The poor get poorer and so do the well-to-do. Inflation, the only way the political schemers have of ''financing'' their schemes, drastically curbs the value of savings. These disguisers succeed in deceiving millions of citizens and, thus, are the enemies of freedom and the good society.

Sometimes thou dost wear the face of pity. This is to say that the victims of vanity think of themselves as virtuous when they sympathize with those in distress. This allows such persons to think they are something they are not— superior to those less fortunate.

Sometimes of generosity. Francois de La Rochefoucauld, French courtier and novelist (1613–80): ''What seems to be generosity is often no more than disguised ambition which overlooks a small interest in order to secure a great one.'' Generosity is a laudable virtue and when practiced brings appreciation and praise. This explains why those who are vanity stricken resort to imitating virtues they do not possess. Showy ambitions, no less!

Many sages have commented on the showy ambitions that thwart and baffle mankind. The American clergyman Henry Ward Beecher (1813–87): ''When a man has no longer any conception of excellence above his own, his voyage is done; he is dead; dead in the trespasses of blear-eyed vanity.'' Suppose I had no conception of excellence beyond my own. I couldn't write this sentence without countless things I know not how to make.

An important question: Why do politicians, as well as many people in other walks of life, "think" they know how to run your and my lives? They are afflicted with *blear-eyed vanity!* Thanks, Henry Ward Beecher, for your phrasing. It lights the road to virtue!

That remarkable thinker and devotee of freedom, Adam Smith, lends credence to the above: "Vanity is the foundation of the most *ridiculous and contemptible vices*—the vices of affectation and common lying."

Adam Smith wasn't alone in his thought about vanity.

> Sin has many tools, but a lie is the handle that fits them all.   —*O. W. Holmes*

> When thou art obliged to speak, be sure to speak the truth; for equivocation is half way to lying and lying is whole way to hell.   —*William Penn*

Speaking truth as one envisions it is a sublime, lofty quality. The English divine, William Robertson (1816–53) gave his contemporaries and those of us in today's world a laudable formula: "*Truth lies in character.* Christ did not simply speak the truth. *He was the truth;* truth through and through; for truth is a thing not of words, but of life and being."

There are a few, including some religious leaders, who share my view that the Second Coming does not mean the coming of another Christ, but rather an attempt of each individual to approximate His Perfection every day of life!

The Irish satirist Jonathan Swift (1667–1745) said about vanity: "The strongest passions allow us some rest but vanity keeps us perpetually in motion. What a dust do I raise! says the fly upon the coachwheel. And what a rate do I drive!

says the fly upon the horse's back.'' On another occasion this author wrote: ''Our passions are like convulsion fits, which, though they make us stronger for the time, leave us the weaker ever after.''

Passion, as here used, is ''the state or power of receiving or being affected by outside influences: condition of being worked upon.''

The English poet Alexander Pope (1688–1744) tells us: ''The general cry is against ingratitude, but the complaint is misplaced, it should be against vanity; none but direct villains are capable of willful ingratitude; but almost everybody is capable of thinking he hath done more than another deserves, while the other thinks he hath received less than he deserves.''

Why cry about faults, moral weaknesses? Might as well cry about those who couldn't care less about politico-economic matters—asleep at the switch, as we say.

Politicians ''think'' they have done for us more than we deserve. And citizens by the millions in their naivete ''think'' they deserve more than the largess they now receive.

Away with vanity! Let us improve our thinking to that point where we are aware of our countless blessings!

The French mathematician and philosopher, Blaise Pascal (1623–62), warned: ''We are so presumptuous that we wish to be known to all the world, even those who come after us; and we are so vain that the esteem of five or six persons immediately around us is enough to amuse and satisfy us.'' Pascal, a wise philosopher, assuredly did not think of himself as among those I'd call sloppy exhibitionists. He used ''we'' to point to a common human trait of presuming to seek fame for the little we do.

The Father of our Country, George Washington, said: "There is no restraining men's tongues or pens when charged with a little vanity." Reflect on those afflicted with vanity, not knowing that they know not, who babble with their tongues and scribble with their pens. This malady, be-like-me-ism, when and if it bedevils a majority of the population, results in know-it-alls being elected to political office. Result? A decline toward all-out socialism!

Washington gave to Americans the thought that when understood and adhered to downs vanity and puts virtue in its place: "Labor to keep alive in your heart that little spark of celestial fire called conscience." And this: "If, to please the people, we offer what we ourselves disapprove, how can we afterwards defend our work? Let us raise a standard to which the wise and honest can repair. The event is in the hand of God."

Those who seek "to please the people" are hungry for popularity. They will promise anything to get votes. These politicians may gain some immediate success, but they bring about ultimate ruin. The statesman, on the other hand, stands by his principles even when they are unpopular. He may thus lose the next election, but his cause is right and will eventually triumph. May we have more statesmen like George Washington!

5

THE LIMITS OF KNOWLEDGE

*Philosophy has been called the
knowledge of our knowledge; it might
more truly be called the knowledge
of our ignorance, or in the language
of Kant, the knowledge of the limits
of our knowledge.* —**MAX MÜLLER**

Rudyard Kipling (1865–1936), set forth in verse the sources
of his wisdom:

> I had six honest serving men
>   Who taught me all I knew
> Their names were Where and What and When
>   and Why and How and Who.

An inquisitive mind, then, is the key to knowledge. For none
of us knows very much. According to Socrates: "That man
thinks he knows everything whereas he knows nothing. I,
on the other hand, know nothing but I know I know nothing."

This, at first blush, seems a strange saying to come from
Socrates who has the reputation of being the wisest of all

19

men. There is, however, an explanation: The more one knows, the greater is the awareness of not knowing. To illustrate:

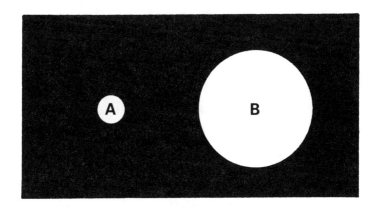

A—one's light—knowing—ten years ago.
B—today: the knowing has increased.

Observe the expanded circumference and note how much more *darkness*—the unknown—confronts the growing person ten years later, and the point is clear! There was little awareness of the *unknown* ten years ago; today it is greatly magnified!

Many wise men, along with Socrates, were aware of how little we know. Four samplings:

> The first step to knowledge is to know that we are ignorant.   *—Richard Cecil*

> We know accurately when we know little; with knowledge doubt increases.   *—Goethe*

He fancies himself enlightened because he sees the deficiencies of others; he is ignorant because he has never reflected on his own.   —*Edward Bulwer-Lytton*

He that boasts of his own knowledge proclaims his ignorance.   —*Thomas Fuller*

I quote once again Thomas Alva Edison: "No one knows more than one-millionth of one per cent of anything." This is no exaggeration. Knowledge at the human level is but an infinitesimal fraction of Creation—there is mystery in everything from the 1,000,000,000,000,000,000,000,000,000 atoms in each human being to galaxies moving away from each other at the speed of light. Except for the know-it-all, all is mystery!

However, we must not let our acknowledged ignorance cast our lives in gloom and despondency. Our opportunities are unbounded. The road to human glory? Seek enlightenment, for it is light that brings forth the eye. Wrote James Thomson (1700–48): "Light! Nature's resplendent robe; without whose vesting beauty all were wrapt in gloom."

Wrote Emerson: "Our knowledge is the amassed thought and experience of innumerable minds." Edith Hamilton gave to posterity one of countless examples—wisdom of the past gracing our lives:

This full stature of greatness came to pass at a time when the mighty civilizations of the ancient world had perished and the shadow of "effortless barbarism" was dark upon the earth. In that black and fierce world a little centre of white-hot spiritual energy was at work. A new civilization had arisen in Athens, unlike all that had gone before.

Wrote the English physicist, John Tyndall (1820–93): "Knowledge once gained casts a light beyond its boundaries."

Reflect on the light—wisdom—given to us by sages, past and present—Socrates, Emerson and countless others. The lesson for you and me? Let us light our candles so brightly that a few others will look to our lights. There is not enough darkness in the whole world to put out the light of one wee candle!

A concluding enlightenment by the English educator Thomas Arnold (1795–1842): "Real knowledge, like everything of value, is not to be attained easily. It must be worked for, studied for, thought for, and, more than all, must be prayed for." This excellent formula needs no commentary by me or anyone else. Creation dwells far off from any of us. Prayer, however, brings creativity to us and links its power to all worthy effort. So, let us pray for liberty, and peace on earth.

6

POVERTY HAS ITS ADVANTAGES

*Of all the advantanges which come
to any young man, I believe it to be
demonstrably true that poverty is the
greatest.* **—JOSIAH G. HOLLAND**

My encyclopedia gives no evidence that this American journalist and author had personally experienced poverty. Therefore, I must assume that he observed men and women born in poverty who had no choice but hard work. Result? Success!

Here are several examples of individuals born in poverty who, as the years advanced, became famous or wealthy. Andrew Carnegie, born a poor lad, became one of our country's greatest entrepreneurs and, by reason of his wealthy and charitable instincts, an outstanding philanthropist. He gave to posterity this gem: "Look out for the boy who has to plunge into work direct from the common school and who begins by sweeping out the office. He is probably the dark horse you had better watch."

Thomas Edison was born in poverty. As a youngster he sold newspapers on a train. Later? The greatest inventive genius of all time—and wealthy!

Abraham Lincoln had only a few months of schooling. Poverty? He was able to purchase from others only a few books. This situation stimulated hard work and superior thinking. Result? One of the greatest Presidents in American history!

A striking example: The Roman Emperor, Domitian (A.D. 51–96), like all despots, then and now, suffered an abysmal ignorance parading as infinite wisdom. In his ''wisdom'' he exiled a slave: Epictetus. Yet so brilliant was this slave's light that it mirrored its way down through fifteen centuries, illuminating such philosophers as Grotius, Kant, Adam Smith, Adam Ferguson and many others.

At first he was a stranger to me, and then came the light. I had read the books of Adam Smith and the others before I knew that the slave's remarkable thinking was the genesis of much of their thinking. Theirs was the philosophy which tended to terminate poverty and political slavery. Glory be to Epictetus and the fame he honestly earned! Domitian and his ilk? They stimulated a reaction which resulted in an overcoming of their harmful practices.

An experience here at FEE fourteen years ago demonstrated that a right tactic can turn a Marxian socialist into a free-market devotee. This man was a lawyer from another country, attending a FEE Seminar. After attending several lectures he announced that FEE's free market, private ownership, limited government philosophy was not for him. He frankly admitted his preference for socialism.

Since FEE is not a reform school we would normally,

under these circumstances, return his tuition and bid the man a fond adieu—as was done with two of his fellow students. However, we made an exception in his case because (1) he expressed a desire to remain, (2) he did not intrude his socialistic views into the discussion and (3) he had a most pleasant and gracious personality, attractive in manner and behavior. So he remained as an auditor.

And then the miracle! A FEE lecturer made a routine explanation of how the free market in action works its wonders in promoting the general prosperity and overcoming poverty. Our foreign friend came to life and saw the light, and exclaimed, "Why you folks are *for* the poor people." He returned to his country and became a leading spokesman for liberty!

It was always one of my ambitions to become "the dark horse you had better watch." Am I qualified? In one respect, yes, for I was born a poor lad. And while in a common school I worked 110 hours each week; among my daily chores was sweeping out two stores in my little town.

I seek neither fame nor wealth. My overriding purpose in life is to improve day in and day out in understanding and explaining the miracles wrought when all of us are free to act creatively as each pleases!

I am seeking a brighter light than I now possess, one that will rid our country of the darkness socialism imposes. Not knowing much, and knowing how little I know—humility— I see my role to be identical to that of the great Spanish philosopher, Jose Ortega y Gasset: "We are going to look for a little of that light. You can expect nothing more, of course. I can only give what I have. Let others who can do more do their more, as I do my little." Many others have shared their "more" with me that my own wee candle may be brightened. This is the stairway to the dispelling of darkness and the light in which freedom appears to be a way of life.

Why do so many well-off individuals think of themselves as poor? They have all the food they wish, clothes for every occasion, vacations when desired, a car to drive, air flight from home to wherever. The answer? They can't keep up with the jet set. They are wealthy, but envy keeps them ignorant of the fact. Wrote the American educator, Bronson Alcott (1799–1888): "To be ignorant of one's ignorance is the malady of ignorance." These poor souls, ignorant of the fact that they are thousands of times wealthier than Cro-Magnon man of 35,000 years ago, and wealthier than Kings prior to England's Industrial Revolution, are to be pitied rather than scorned.

Let me conclude with a few thoughts on poverty which may be enlightening to those who are unaware of their material blessings.

I turn first to the Greek philosopher Plutarch (46–120): "Poverty is not dishonorable in itself, but only when it comes from idleness, intemperance, extravagance and folly." What foresight! This Greek lived in poverty, that is, compared to those of our day who "think" of themselves as poverty stricken. Plutarch never dreamed of the planes by which we travel or of automobiles, telephones, electric lights, railroads, buzz saws or countless other material comforts that bless our lives. But he was aware of the vices that make poverty dishonorable.

The Athenian statesman Pericles (495–429 B.C.) spoke of poverty and its cure: "Not to be able to bear poverty is a shameful thing; but not to know how to chase it away by work is a more shameful thing yet." This is in accord with Carnegie's testimony to the value of work!

The American journalist Arthur Brisbane (1864–1936) shared this view: "Nations like men can be healthy and happy, though comparatively poor. Wealth is a means to an end, not the end itself." As I have written over and over again, wealth is a means to rid self of mundane chores in order that one may be freed for creative activity.

Oliver Goldsmith (1728–1774) found that: "Want of prudence is too frequently the want of virtue; nor is there on earth a more powerful advocate for vice than poverty." Millions who classify themselves as poor succeed in getting government to subsidize them. They live by the Marxian scheme: "From each according to his ability, to each according to his need." In essence, they are robbing Peter to pay Paul. Result? Inflation increasing annually. What a vice! If inflation is not halted everyone will be reduced to poverty!

If we are truly concerned for the poor, let us halt the political intervention and open to everyone the opportunities and blessings of freedom.

7

THE ENJOYMENT OF TRUTH

There are three parts in truth; first,
the inquiry, which is the wooing of
it; secondly, the knowledge of it,
which is the presence of it; and thirdly,
the belief, which is the enjoyment of
it. **—FRANCIS BACON**

Most of us are truly gratified if we are blest with a single
creative talent. Francis Bacon (1561–1626) excelled most
sages. He was graced by being not only a jurist but also a
scientist, author, philosopher, and a member of Parliament.
Those of us who are seekers of truth might well ponder his
views on the matter.

It is interesting to note what several thoughtful individuals
have had to say about the three steps to the enjoyment of
truth: (1) inquiry, (2) knowledge, (3) belief. As to inquiry,
the Swiss divine and historian J. H. M. D'Aubigne (1794–
1872) made this observation:

> Free inquiry, if restrained within due bounds, and ap-
> plied to proper subjects, is a most important privilege of

the human mind; and if well conducted, is one of the greatest friends to truth. But when reason knows neither its office nor its limits, and when employed on subjects foreign to its jurisdiction it then becomes a privilege dangerous to be exercised.

Now and always keep in mind D'Aubigne's profound thought: Free inquiry "applied to proper subjects, is a most important privilege of the human mind." One of several "proper subjects" is freedom.

Ralph Waldo Emerson gave to posterity an excellent thought on the importance of inquiry: "Be content with a little light, so it be your own. *Explore and explore and explore.* Be neither chided nor flattered out of your position of *perpetual inquiry.* Neither dogmatize, nor accept another's dogmatism. Truth has its roof, and bed, and board. Make yourself necessary to the world, and mankind will give you bread."

We should, indeed, be content with a little light, a human portion. No individual, past or present, has been graced with more than a smattering of knowledge, that is, when compared to Infinite Consciousness. But it is fidelity to this glimmer on the part of finite individuals that sparks evolution—the good life! To avoid destroying our creative role requires that we never dogmatize—never be a dictocrat, nor heed their nonsense. This dreadful error is the intellectual slayer of Truth! Explore and explore and explore! To explore is the wooing of Truth!

Now to *knowledge.* Wrote George Washington:

It is substantially true, that virtue or morality is a necessary spring of popular government. The rule indeed extends with more or less force to every species of free government. Who that is a sincere friend to it, can look with indifference upon attempts to shake the foundation of the fabric. Promote then as an object of primary importance, institutions for the general diffusion of knowledge. In proportion as the structure of a government gives force to public opinion, it is essential that public opinion be enlightened.

Imagine no self-governed individuals, no self-control exercised by anyone, everybody running around hog wild, as we say. With no self-imposed restraints, the situation could be likened to a rabble of madmen or imbeciles. Liberty? None whatsoever!

The very first step in knowing how to use our liberty is the practice of self-government. What is the key to this discipline, the mastery of pride? It is humility, the essential foundation of virtue. Liberty is possible only when men know how to and do, in fact, govern themselves!

Ponder these thoughts:

1—To improve yourself you must be free.
2—Your contribution depends on the use you make of your liberty.
3—Only a highly evolved man is willing to defend the equal liberty of all others!

There is no short cut to evolution!

Washington referred to "institutions for the general diffusion of knowledge"—the freedom our Founding Fathers so courageously documented and stood for. I believe that FEE is an example of what George Washington had in mind—an organization devoting itself *exclusively* to freedom principles since its founding in 1946. The harvest of our efforts?

Many organizations have come into existence as a result of FEE's work: competitors, each trying to excel all others. Why is this good? In competing we learn from each other. Competitive/cooperative effort by growing numbers of freedom devotees will lead our country away from the growing socialism, along the freedom freeway of life!

Wrote Goethe: "Man is not made to solve the problems of the universe, but to find out what he has to do; and to restrain himself within the limits of his comprehension." Solve the problems of the universe? Never! No man is capable of solving the problems of his village, let alone the problems of his city, or state, or nation. His assignment is to enlighten himself. This is within the limits of his comprehension; this is what he should do. Let him grow sufficiently in knowledge and others will seek his tutorship. Improving individuals constitute the genesis of an improving universe, in America and elsewhere.

Finally, to *belief*. Wrote the American psychologist William James (1842–1910): "These, then, are my last words to you: Be not afraid of life. Believe that life is worth living and you will help locate the facts." Emerson further enlightens us on the life worth living: "Life is a series of surprises. We do not guess today the mood, the pleasure, the power of tomorrow when we are building up our being."

How do we overcome fear of life? By increasing our awareness of our countless blessings! I count my birth as blessing number one. Every breath is a blessing, as is every heart beat, and eyes to see, ears to hear. Countless blessings from William James, Emerson, Confucius, Socrates and other sages who inspire creative thinking.

Our Founding Fathers a blessing? Indeed, yes, for had it

not been for them I would be a mere serf—a servant to Kings, Lords, and others of the authoritarian ilk. Never to be omitted among my blessings are the trillions of creative, inventive thoughts flowing to my advantage. One of ever so many examples: I can send my voice around the world in one-seventh of a second! Such achievements are among my blessings. Other everyday miracles free me from all mundane, common, everyday chores, and I am graced with the opportunity to devote myself—while living in relative luxury—to my one highest aspiration: working at the one ambition I love: freedom!

To seek the truth of freedom, and to believe it, is the highest enjoyment.

8

SEVERAL FACETS OF FREEDOM

The only freedom which deserves the name, is that of pursuing our own good in our own way, so long as we do not attempt to deprive others of theirs, or impede their efforts to obtain it. **—JOHN STUART MILL**

The quotation from Mill's famed essay, *On Liberty,* published in 1859, captures the essence of freedom. But there are many facets or aspects of the subject that merit elaboration. And my purpose here is to enlarge upon some of these facets.

Knowledge. If individuals somehow could be ranked according to how much each knows, and if each were then asked to list those things unknown to him, it is likely that the best informed would also have the longest list of "unknowns."

The recognition on the part of Socrates that he knew nothing but that he knew he knew nothing—the first step toward wisdom—is, from the standpoint of human freedom and prosperity the most important recognition there is. Why?

Each of us has an infinitesimal bit of knowledge—limited expertise at this or that. When the market is free—no restrictions against production and exchange—the tiny bits of know-how possessed by millions of discrete individuals flow naturally and easily, contributing to the prosperity of each. This knowledge is in the market process itself, not in you or me or anyone else—the claims of the know-it-alls to the contrary notwithstanding. To paraphrase the thought of a great philosopher: Man is not born to solve the problems of the universe but, rather, to find out what he can best do. Knowing this is knowledge at the human level.

It is in freedom that one's knowledge is put to best human use.

Excellence. It is not mere quantity of knowledge that counts, for even the most knowledgeable man among us has a mere glimpse of all that is to be known; he has but lit a wee candle in a vast darkness. The individual who counts is the one who is growing in knowledge, for excellence includes growth. Call it the aristocratic spirit, as did Hanford Henderson:

> He may be a day laborer, an artisan, a shopkeeper, a professional man, a writer, a statesman. It is not a matter of birth, or occupation, or education. It is an attitude of mind carried into daily action . . . a religion. It is the disinterested, passionate love of excellence . . . everywhere and in everything; the aristocrat, to deserve the name, must love it in himself, in his own alert mind, in his own illuminated spirit, and he must love it in others; must love it in all human relations and occupations and activities; in all things in earth or sea or sky.

Jefferson added his thought: "There is a natural aristocracy among men; it is composed of virtues and talents."

When the aristocratic spirit is in ascendancy, the keynote of which is *excellence,* freedom reigns!

Influence. There is no fraction so small that it is not divisible, and no heartbeat but is felt throughout the universe—there is no action we take—good or bad—that fails to exert an influence on someone. Thus, the question: How influence others better to understand and explain the free society? The answer: Let anyone who would move mankind toward freedom *first move himself!*

Persons capable of enlightenment will seek light only from the already enlightened. The lesson? Never try to reform another; do not try to forcibly draw others toward your view. Instead, strive for that perfection of understanding and exposition which will cause them to do the reaching. There is an infallible guideline in this matter: observe whether others are seeking your tutorship. If not, there's homework to be done. Goethe shares his wisdom:

> He who wishes to exert a useful influence must be careful to insult nothing. Let him not be troubled by what seems absurd, but concentrate his energies to the creation of what is good. He must not demolish, but *build.* He must raise temples where mankind may come and partake of the purest pleasures.

Through the better personal practice of freedom may we attract others to share its blessings.

Merit. Merit, if it be genuine, cannot be concealed. "There is not enough darkness in the whole world to put out the light of one wee candle." As Albert Jay Nock suggested, the Remnant—those who are seeking light, the ones who really count—will find true merit. It cannot be hidden for long.

But merit can be depreciated by putting it on exhibit—"What a great man am I." Instead of looking to him for light, the common reaction is to shun the person who blatantly "toots his own horn."

History reveals that contemporaries see more the man than his merit. Posterity, on the other hand, sees only the merit and not the man. We have never seen Confucius, Socrates, Goethe, Emerson and other greats of the past, but we can see and respect their merit. We do not see the authors of freedom; however, more and more of us are coming to see the merit of their work.

Competition. Many among us insist that man is born for cooperation, not competition—as if these were antagonistic to one another. Such people readily see the blessings of cooperation, but they fail to realize that cooperation is only a dream in the absence of competition.

Genuine competition implies rules, such as the rule of free entry. Free entry in any field of endeavor—the production of goods or the supplying of services or whatever—assures competition, each participant trying to excel. Free competition among suppliers results in cooperation with customers. Examples: When there is real competition among the bakers of bread, we customers decide whose bread we eat, that is, with whom we will cooperate.

The goal of competition in the free market is to serve customers better, according to consumer choice. The alternative is coercion applied by those who would have the field exclusively to themselves. Such enslavement of others is a process of stagnation, rather than growth. And such a coercive society affords no incentive for self-improvement.

When there is competition, there are always those out front, setting the pace, leading the way. The effect of this leadership? Others have the desire to improve their rank and, thus, are inspired to grow. Competition—trying to excel— is the origin of growth; it is the *magnet* that draws forth each man's best in the practice of freedom!

Justice. Government, the political arm or agent of society, can have no higher aim than justice for one and all alike. The Goddess of Justice is blindfolded; her concern is not with who you are but, rather, with how fairly and honestly one deals with one's fellowmen. Justice conforms to such ideals as:

- The Golden Rule.
- The principle of universality; that is, avoid any action that would bring ruin and chaos if universally practiced.
- No special privilege for anyone.
- No violation of the right to the fruits of one's own labor or the right to act creatively as one chooses.

Optimism. Nature presents us with contrasts: light and dark, hot and cold, calm and blizzards, the ebb and flow of tides, greenery and deserts, oscillations on and on.

Man enters the earthly scene and adds oscillations galore: depressions and "good times," dark ages and renaissance periods, starvation and plenitude, dictatorship and freedom, and so forth.

"Isn't this an awful day," says the person who finds the weather not to his fancy. Likewise, seeing only a decline and fall and absurdities of all sorts in society, a person may vigorously denounce the bad while failing to see the good. This is pessimism, which fails to advance the good.

On the other hand is the person who realizes that it is always darkest before the dawn, that there is a silver lining in every cloud, that the good is in the offing. He stands foursquare for his belief—his faith that the right will prevail. This is optimism which advances the good.

Optimism does not mean a blindness to what happens, or fancy notions about a rosy future. Rather, it is a belief that there's a good day coming and that by emphasizing this belief the good will become a reality—sooner! Here rests the case for faith in freedom.

9

EDUCATION FOR VIRTUE

We have in America the largest public school system on earth, the most expensive college buildings, the most expensive curriculum, but nowhere else is education so blind to its objectives, so indifferent to any specific outcome as in America. One trouble has been its negative character. It has aimed at the repression of faults rather than the creation of virtue.

—WILLIAM H. P. FAUNCE

Faunce (1859–1930), an educator and clergyman, became President of Brown University in 1899. My encyclopedia says of him: "A champion of the liberal arts curriculum . . . in his 30-year administration placed Brown among the leading American Universities."

I have no way of knowing whether President Faunce was aware of how public, that is, government, education may very well have had its root in Napoleon's dictatorial views such as, "Public instruction should be the first object of

39

government." What follows is a briefing of what I wrote in a book four years ago:

> Napoleon now merged the various institutions of learning in a new University of France *under officials* nominated and supervised by the executive power. . . . "No one," it was decreed, "may open a school or teach publicly unless he is a member of the imperial university."[1]

If this be the root, then this may be the sequence of its transplanting here. Our brilliant Thomas Jefferson invited his close friend, the brilliant Pierre Samuel du Pont de Nemours, to study and recommend an appropriate form of education for the U.S.A. Du Pont wrote a 161-page book,[2] and Jefferson proceeded to implement its conclusion. Public education!

Why du Pont, a physiocrat and at odds with Napoleon on every other matter, should arrive at such a recommendation is difficult to understand, except that he lived a good part of his life in that "educational" atmosphere. Neither Jefferson nor his friend could see the scraggly bush that would grow from these roots.

The scraggly bush did not show up until well in the twentieth century. But now it is growing by leaps and bounds—and so are costs. In a district not far from FEE the taxpayers are forced to pay over $4,000 per student for nine months of "schooling."

I, along with numerous freedom devotees, am unequivo-

---

[1]See *History of Western Education* by William Boyd (London: Adam & Charles Black, 1950), p. 360.

[2]*National Education in the United States of America* (Newark, Delaware: University of Delaware Press, 1923).

cally opposed to government "education" and stand four-square for private education. But what a dilemma this presents! Why? There are countless teachers in private schools, colleges and universities who advocate the planned economy and the welfare state—Socialism! And I am acquainted with numerous teachers in government schools who are teaching the private ownership, free market, limited government way of life—Freedom!

What, then, in this confusion, is your and my role? What can the remedy be? Daniel Webster, American orator and statesman (1782–1852) gave to posterity a sound and virtuous formula:

> Knowledge does not comprise all which is contained in the large term of education. The feelings are to be disciplined; the passions are to be restrained; true and worthy motives are to be inspired; a profound religious feeling is to be instilled, and pure morality inculcated under all circumstances. All this is comprised in education.

The French astronomer and mathematician, Pierre Laplace (1749–1827) added this thought: "What we know here is very little but what we are ignorant of is immense." I confess to knowing very little about my greatest aspiration, namely, explaining with clarity how the free and unfettered market works its miracles. No one excels me in conviction, but difficulty in finding words and phrasings to transmit the great truths about freedom to others accounts for my shortcomings.

But what we are ignorant of is immense. Of course, we cannot explain the unknown; but we can marvel at the vastness of it—and keep searching.

Any thoughtful person must agree with Webster, namely, that education worthy of the name requires that our feelings be disciplined, and passions restrained. Instead, all true and worthy motives are to be inspired, the springboard of which is the aspiration for intellectual, moral and spiritual improvement.

Here is what a few among many wise men have written that supports and clarifies Webster's views on religion. The American patriot, Josiah Quincy (1744–75):

> The great comprehensive truths, written in letters of living light on every page of our history, are these: Human happiness *has no perfect security but freedom;* freedom none but virtue; virtue none but knowledge; and neither freedom nor virtue has any vigor or immortal hope except in the principles of the Christian faith, and in the sanctions of the Christian religion.

America was founded on the Truth that the Creator is the endower of all rights to life and livelihood, thus, unseating government from that role. Result? The greatest outburst of creativity in all history! Unfortunately, more and more citizens have forgotten the source of our plenitude.

The English banker and philanthropist Samuel Montague (1832–1911) told us: "Christianity is the good man's test, His life is the illustration. How admirable is that religion, which, while it seems to have in view only the felicity of another world, is at the same time the highest happiness of this."

Edmund Burke adds this thought: "We know, and what is better, we feel inwardly, that religion is the basis of civil society, and the source of all good and of all comfort." This truth is well demonstrated in the work of our Founding Fathers!

Ever so many individuals assess themselves as educated at the time of high school or college graduation. This "thought" is a contradiction of human evolution. Education should continue throughout one's life. Indeed, whenever growth in awareness, perception, consciousness terminates, life's highest purpose is at a dead end.

This belief is founded on my own experience. As to education in its commonly accepted sense, I concluded mine at high school. It was obvious to me that compared to many of my acquaintances I did not know much.

What to do? I sought tutors, men far out front intellectually, morally, spiritually. How did I win their tutorship? By confessing my ignorance and pleading for their help. Result? Without exception, enlightening responses! Further, I have sought enlightenment from the outstanding sages of the past. A laudable ambition? Faunce set forth the goal: *Aim at the creation of virtues!*

10

MY RIGHTS ARE YOUR RIGHTS

*Whatever each man can separately
do, without trespassing on the rights
of others, he has a right to do for
himself; and he has a right to a fair
portion of all which society, with all
its combination of skill and force can
do in his favor. In this partnership all
men have equal rights; but not to
equal things.* **—EDMUND BURKE**

Burke (1729–97) and Adam Smith (1723–90), two of the
world's wisest as politico-economic thinkers, and ramrod
straight in their moral principles, were contemporaries.
Doubtless, they learned from each other. In any event, each
of them played an important role in the founding of the
United States of America.

My aim in this essay is to comment on man—any individual—and his relation to others, past and present, with the
hope of finding thoughts that will assure an improving future. Longfellow proved himself to be a real sage in the
following: "Look not mournfully to the past—it comes not
back again; wisely move to the present—it is divine; go
forth to meet the shadowy future without fear, and with a
manly heart."

Ever so many devotees of freedom reflect mournfully on

the past eight decades, which have witnessed our decline into socialism. Why so saddened? They assess our sociological slump as having no turnabout possibilities: "It comes not back again." Move to the present! The pendulum that swung freely to the left, having reached its limit, swings as freely to the right.

"It is divine." Yes, it is ordained in the Cosmic Design—evolution moving onward and upward over the centuries. Briefly, have no fear of the shadowy future. Replace fear with a manly heart—optimism. We are going to win sooner or later, that is, if there be enough manly hearts. I am an optimist as are so many others. A few examples follow.

The American clergyman Ezra Hall Gillett (1823–75): "We are always looking to the future; the present does not satisfy us. Our ideal, whatever it may be, lies further on."

The ideal always lies "further on." Tryon Edwards enlightens those of us seeking truth: "We never reach our ideals, whether of mental or moral improvement, but the thought of them shows us our deficiencies, and spurs us on to higher and better things."

Those of us who have the freedom way of life among our ideals realize the absolute necessity of mental and moral improvement. And the more we advance in this respect, the more we know that there is more to know. Our goal of creativity at the human level has no stopping point. What then? Strive for a closer approximation, now and forever!

Ralph Waldo Emerson said: "Mankind has ever been divided into two sects, Materialists and Idealists; the first founded on experience, the second on consciousness." I assume that the Sage of Concord meant by Materialists those who specialize in goods and services, where success is, for the most part, founded on experience. Those up topside serve consumers remarkably. They become our servants in ever so many ways! Consciousness? An awareness of righteousness, mankind's eternal reality!

Ralph Waldo Trine, who wrote *In Tune With the Infinite,* was in tune with Emerson: "Everything is first worked out in the unseen before it is manifested in the seen, *in the ideal* before it is realized in the real, in the spiritual before it shows forth *in the material.*"

The spiritual? The late Ludwig von Mises, one of the world's greatest economists, gave us the correct answer:

> Production is a spiritual, intellectual and ideological phenomenon. It is the method that man, directed by reason, employs for the best possible removal of uneasiness. What distinguishes our conditions from those of our ancestors who lived one thousand or twenty thousand years ago is not something material but something spiritual. The material changes are the outcome of the spiritual changes.

Whenever the spiritual shows forth in the material the results are far more than is generally realized. About 400 years ago the population in this land of ours was estimated to be no more than 1,000,000. Why? Lack of natural resources? There were more then than now.

The Indians lived by foraging—a primitive society. An absence of Materialists! It was the coming of the Materialists that accounts for our present population approximating 220,000,000. Had this not been the case, the chances are 220 to one that neither you nor I would have been born. So hail to the spiritual, the Idealists, that gave and still give birth to the Materialists!

Edward H. Chapin comments on the mystery of life: "To me there is something exalting in the thought that we are drifting forward into a splendid mystery, into something that no mortal eye has yet seen, and no intelligence has yet declared." Everything in this mortal life verges into mystery. Every one of us has but dim notions of what has happened in the last minute and not the slightest idea of what will happen in the next year—or minute. We are forever faced with the unknown. How wonderful, were more of us to realize that "we are drifting forward into a splendid mystery." This is an optimism ordained by Creation: evolution in awareness, perception, consciousness!

Albert Einstein believed in the mysterious, along with Chapin, yours truly and, hopefully, your good self:

The most beautiful thing we can experience is the mysterious. It is the source of all true art and science. He to whom this emotion is a stranger, who can no longer pause to wonder and stand rapt in awe, is as good as dead: his eyes are closed. To know that what is impenetrable to us really exists, manifesting itself as the highest wisdom and the most radiant beauty which our dull facilities can comprehend . . . is at the center of true religion.

Finally, a reflection on Burke's wisdom. When one specializes in freedom and its mysteries, there is no trespassing on the rights of others. The same applies to everyone, regardless of specialization. All citizens have an equal right to pursue their respective aspirations, but no right to "equal things." I have no right to your reward, nor you to mine. Thus, my rights are your rights so long as they are creative.

11

FEARLESS AND FREE

You must conquer fear or be a slave.
No slave chains or iron bars are as
restricting as fear. It is ridiculous for
one to talk about "America, the land
of the free and the home of the brave"
while he wears the ball and chain of
fear. **—LEROY BROWNLOW**

The above appears in a remarkable book, *Today Is Mine,* an inspirational guide to living by the President of the Brownlow Publishing Company.[1] Following the above, he adds a warning all of us should heed: "No person is free who is afraid to try lest he fail; or who fears to break with tradition; or who is scared to stand for right when in its ranks there are only the few; or who is frightened to speak the truth when the masses hold to error; or who is too chicken-hearted to be his own master."

Reflect on those who fear to explore what is unknown to them. They are frightened by the thought of failure and remain dormant—life's mission abandoned. Fear to break with tradition? Our nation's tradition for the past eight decades has been nothing less than the observed decline toward so-

---

[1]P.O. Box 3141, Fort Worth, Texas 76105.

cialism. Millions are frightened at the thought of defying a movement which is so popular. They are scared to join the very few of us who espouse the freedom way of life. Follow the minority? No, they say! The majority? Yes! Mere "tag alongs"!

Frightened to speak the truth when the masses hold to error? Yes, too chicken-hearted to be one's own master. Such chickens have been ruling the roost!

Today Is Mine is a book of daily readings for an entire year. Brownlow's subject for each day is introduced by a quotation from some wise man and concluded by a bit of wisdom from the Holy Bible. Here are one day's quotations.

The wise man: The American literary critic, poet and humorist James Russell Lowell (1819–91):

> They are slaves who fear to speak
> For the fallen and the weak;
> They are slaves who will not choose
> Hatred, scoffing, and abuse,
> Rather than in silence shrink
> From the truth they needs must think;
> They are slaves who dare not be
> In the right with two or three.

The Holy Bible: "I was afraid . . . and I hid myself."

Lowell was not referring to the despicable Negro slavery of early America but to an enslaved mentality, a dormancy of the mind—all creative thoughts in cold storage! He condemned those who fear to speak truth against popular jargon—gibberish! Doubtless, it was this mental depravity which accounted for the Negro slavery that all intelligent citizens despise.

It is interesting to note the variety of ideas wise men have had about fear. Some examples and, now and then, a commentary. The English mathematician and philosopher Bertrand Russell (1872–1970): "Our instinctive emotions are those we have inherited from a much more dangerous world, and contain, therefore, a larger portion of fear than they should."

Go back five or six generations. Our ancestors had no transportation except horse-or-oxen-drawn vehicles, and little control over nature. Life was hazardous. The result of crop failures? Starvation! Many in today's world, those who have no inkling of how the free market works its wonders, have inherited "a larger portion of fear than they should." Diseases took their toll. Pneumonia, smallpox, and other plagues wiped out thousands in each generation. Today? The cures are known!

The American author and critic Christian N. Bovee (1820–1904): "There is great beauty in going through life without anxiety or fear. Half our fears are baseless and the other half discreditable."

When anxiety or fear dominate one's life, creative thought and action—growth in awareness, perception, consciousness—lie dormant, asleep. True, most fears are baseless, senseless! Discreditable? Yes, they are—to use other adjectives—disgraceful, shoddy, shameful! What may we say of those thus afflicted? *Poor souls!*

Only those who go through life unafflicted by such emotional disturbances can experience the intellectual beauty of advancing freedom for themselves and others. *Rich souls!*

The Greek philosopher Aristotle (384–322 B.C.): "No one loves the man whom he fears." I, for one, do not love the Hitlers, Stalins or other dictocrats abroad or at home. I fear the disaster their know-it-all-ness inflicts on civilization and their thwarting of human evolution. However, I must never pronounce my hate for them. Why? It hardens them in their wayward ways!

Wrote the English poet and statesman George Villiers, Duke of Buckingham (1628–87): "All true love is grounded on esteem." I esteem and thus love freedom devotees.

The American journalist William Allen White (1868–1944): "Put fear out of your heart. This nation will survive, this state will prosper, the orderly business of life will go forward if only men can speak in whatever way given them to utter what their hearts hold—by voice, by postal cards, by letter or by press. Only force and oppression have made the wrecks in the world." Mr. White, Publisher and Editor of the *Emporia Gazette,* Emporia, Kansas, gained national fame with his small-town newspaper and his superior thinking on behalf of liberty. Another thought of his: "Liberty is the only thing you cannot have unless you are willing to give it to others." And he did his best to transmit to others the liberty he so eloquently espoused.

William Allen White grasped the wrong and the right. The wrong? "Only force and oppression have made the wrecks in the world." Oppression, is but another name for "irresponsible power." It is the powermongers who wreck civilization!

The right? White and I see eye to eye on America's future. He was, and I am, an optimist. We, and many others, are not the oppressors. We firmly believe that only the fearless are free.

12

SELF-IMPROVEMENT

Every temptation that is resisted, every noble aspiration that is encouraged, every sinful thought that is repressed, every bitter word that is withheld, adds its little item to the impetus of that great movement which is bearing humanity onward toward a richer life and higher character. **—WILBUR FISK**

The above, by the American divine (1792–1839), is an excellent beginning for the purpose of this essay, namely, an examination of such virtues as self-control, self-examination, self-improvement, and self-knowledge.

As to self-control, Goethe asked an appropriate question and gave a correct answer: "What is the best government? That which teaches us to govern ourselves." This is not to deny the value of properly limited civil government. Were a sufficient number of us to govern ourselves, there would be no demand for government to subsidize and regulate the citizens.

Samuel Smiles added these thoughts: "For the want of self-restraint many men are engaged all their lives in fighting with difficulties of their own making, and rendering success impossible by their own cross-grained ungentleness; whilst others, it may be much less gifted, make their way and achieve success by simple patience, equanimity and self-control." Why do so many spend all their lives in fighting difficulties of their own making? It is as Smiles said, for the lack of self-restraint. The root of this lack? A deadened power to *overcome,* making their *becoming* unlikely; thus unaware of their potentialities which may be great. Many of those less gifted control and overcome this weakness and succeed in achieving their unique potentialities.

The Scottish divine John Caird (1820–98), adds to our enlightenment: "Self-government is, indeed, the noblest role on earth: the object of a loftier ambition than the possession of crowns and scepters. The truest conquest is where the soul is bringing every thought into captivity to the obedience of Christ. The monarch of his own mind is the only real potentate."

Self-government is indeed the noblest role on earth, loftier than crowns. It is an order infinitely higher than that of political dictocrats, who would coercively impose their know-it-all-ness on the citizenry. Such simpletons haven't the slightest idea how the free and unfettered market works its wonders and, thus, are menaces to "the noblest role on earth." Here is an example of such "thinking" by the late Walter Reuther, head of the United Auto Workers for years: "Only a moron would believe that the millions of private economic decisions being made independently of each other will somehow harmonize in the end and bring us out where we want to be." Walter Reuther and his brother Victor had their early "economic" schooling in the U.S.S.R.

Next, a reflection on self-examination. The Roman Stoic philosopher Lucius A. Seneca (4 B.C.–65 A.D.), suggested how each of us might well examine ourselves. "We should every night call ourselves to an account: What infirmity have I mastered today? What passions opposed? What temptations resisted? What virtue acquired? Our vices will abate of themselves if they be brought every day to the shrift." By "every day to the shrift" means a daily confession of our errors. Wrote Saint Augustine, "The confession of evil works is the beginning of good works."

Self-improvement should never be overlooked. Wrote that famous aviator, the late Charles Lindbergh: "The improvement of our way of life is more important than the spreading of it. If we make it satisfactory enough, it will spread automatically. If we do not, no strength of arms can permanently impose it." This emphasizes the folly of trying to ram one's ideas into the minds of others. The right method? Concentrate on the improvement of self. If a person becomes good enough, others will seek his tutorship. If no one seeks you out, there's homework to be done! Strength of arms—political know-it-alls imitating Hitler and his ilk [armed forces]—is debilitating, the opposite of enlightening.

The English novelist Bulwer-Lytton, whom I often quote, observed more than a century ago:

"Know thyself" said the old philosophy. "Improve thyself" said the new. Our great object in time is not to waste our passions and gifts on the things external that we must leave behind, but that we cultivate within us all that we can carry into the eternal progress beyond.

The German scholar Thomas a Kempis (1380–1471), gave us several thoughts to ponder, relating to self-knowledge. "The highest and most profitable learning is the knowledge of ourselves. To have a low opinion of our own merits, and to think highly of others, is an evidence of wisdom. All men are frail, but thou shouldest reckon none so frail as thyself."

Wilbur Fisk believed as I do, that when temptations and other weaknesses are overcome, we are "bearing humanity toward a richer life and higher character." As the Roman, Horace, wrote: "Adversity has the effect of eliciting talents which in prosperous circumstances would have lain dormant." The adversity which we have been experiencing during the past several decades is now eliciting talents that assures a turnabout to *the freedom way of life!*

13

EXALTING THE COMMON GOOD

To sustain the individual freedom of action contemplated by the Constitution is not to strike down the common good, but to exalt it; for surely the good of society as a whole cannot be better served than by the preservation against arbitrary restraint of the liberties of its constituent members.

—GEORGE SUTHERLAND

This statesman, born in England, studied law at the University of Michigan Law School, practiced law in Utah, was a member of the House of Representatives 1901–03, and a Senator 1905–17. He became Associate Justice of the U.S. Supreme Court, serving in that capacity from 1922 to 1938.

Most citizens in today's U.S.A. haven't the slightest understanding of the Declaration of Independence, the Constitution and the Bill of Rights.

Sutherland, on the other hand, understood these writings

as well as did the authors of these politico-economic, spiritual documents: the greatest in all history! The basic premise that separates the American experiment in Man-Government relationships from all others is contained in the second paragraph of the Declaration of Independence:

> We hold these truths to be self-evident, that all men are created equal, that they are endowed by their Creator with certain unalienable Rights, that among these are Life, Liberty, and the pursuit of Happiness. That to secure these rights, Governments are instituted among Men, deriving their just powers from the consent of the governed.

Reflect on the fact that these signers were, for the most part, men of means. Instead of wealth to gain, they were faced with the prospect of losses. What, pray tell, might be the nature of that loss? The likelihood—the possibility—of signing their own death warrant, so contrary to popular opinion were their glorious intentions!

Twenty-four of these men were well-educated lawyers and judges; eleven were merchants of one variety or another; nine were farmers and plantation owners; all were men of means. They were willing to trade their well-being to bring about, at best, the birth of a nation with unprecedented freedom principles; or a dangerous hangman's rope, at worse!

Almost to a man, they paid a heavy price! Nine were reduced to poverty within a short time. Five were captured by the British, imprisoned and died within a few years. Twelve had their homes, farms or plantations sacked, looted by the British. Nine died during the war, either from bullets or personal hardship. Few survived to live out natural lives. They pledged—and they paid—and in doing so they gave birth to your and my freedom. Would you have signed the Declaration? Your answer is affirmative—provided that you are trying, regardless of opposition and unpopularity, to regain the liberty our Founding Fathers bequeathed to us Americans. Hail to their wisdom, courage and exemplarity.[1]

Justice Sutherland insisted that we should exalt the common good, his reference being the *good* set forth in our Constitution. It seems appropriate that I repeat some observations made in one of my earlier books.

What is a miracle? "It is," says the dictionary, "an event or action that apparently contradicts known scientific laws and is hence thought to be due to supernatural causes especially an act of God." Creation!

Why do so few approve, accept and abide by the freedom way of life? A confession: I, along with many others, have been saying, "It is so difficult to explain." The truth as I now see it? *No one can or ever will be able to explain the miracle of freedom.* Were clear, lucid and persuasive explanation a requirement, some one or more of us would need to understand and explain every facet of human action—creativity at the human level. No individual is or ever has been graced with such wisdom. Nor is such omniscience necessary for a belief in freedom.

Everything in Creation, including every form of life—no exception—is a miracle when viewed aright. However, one will seldom find a recording among famous intellectuals—past or present—who will agree with this statement. One notable exception was an English divine Robert South (1634–1716): "A miracle is a work *exceeding the power of any*

[1]Much of the above is taken from a great book, *America's Choice*, by James R. Evans. See a review in *The Freeman*, November 1981.

created agent: consequently, being an effect of the divine omnipotence.''

Many individuals have looked upon freedom, not as a miracle, but as an explainable way of life. Being unable to explain it themselves and knowing of no one who can, they hold it in far less esteem than socialism which they find easier to explain.

All but a few are blind to freedom's miracles. Thomas Alva Edison, perhaps the greatest inventive genius of all time, gave us one explanation of this blindness: ''No one knows more than a millionth of one per cent of anything.'' This, of course, was a figure of speech. He could have said a billionth or trillionth of one per cent. Compared to Infinite Consciousness, finite man is no more than a mere speck in Creation's Domain. Grasping this point—the more one knows the more awareness of how little he knows . . . is the beginning of such wisdom as is within mortal man's domain.

There are reasons galore as to why freedom is not believed to be a miracle. Here is one: Our everyday life is crowded with miracles, so many that they have become commonplace. No one ''contradicts'' them. My telephone is an example. I can send my voice around the world at the speed of light—in one-seventh of a second. While few will think of this recent phenomenon as a miracle, I have never heard anyone say that it is not. No contradiction! During the past few decades millions of miracles, ranging from penicillin to jet airplanes, are taken for granted, accepted as are the miracles of nature, be they blades of grass or giant oaks.

Froude, the English divine (1818–94) wrote: ''The practical effect of a belief is the real test of its soundness.'' Is it practical to believe in the unexplainable miracle, freedom?

The answer is an unequivocal "*Yes.*" Why? Because the individual's freedom to act creatively as he pleases is materially, morally and spiritually sound.

At our down-to-earth level, more miracles than anyone can count result from freedom, the greatest demonstration in all history being the American miracle.

There is one detail that should be explainable but no one to my knowledge has phrased it well enough for effective communication: it has to do with individual differences. Let us find a way to put these facts into understandable terms. No two of us are remotely alike. Indeed, no one individual is the same now as he or she was a moment ago. All is change now and forever. When our tiny bits of expertise are free to flow, they configurate. As drops of water make an ocean, so do these bits make the miracle.

Here are some final thoughts gleaned from that brilliant Frenchman Alexis de Tocqueville (1805–59). First, some background. During the middle years of the last century, numerous governments sent commissions to the U.S.A. to find out why our success and their failures. All of them went home with the wrong answers. Tocqueville, by himself, made the all-important discovery:

> I sought for the greatness and genius of America in fertile fields and boundless forests; it was not there. I sought for it in her institutions of learning; it was not there. I sought for it in her matchless Constitution; it was not there. Not until I went to the churches of America and found them aflame with righteousness did I understand the greatness and genius of America. *America is great because America is good. When America ceases to be good, America will cease to be great.*

A few other thoughts by Tocqueville which lend credence to this thesis:

The soil is productive less by reason of its fertility than because the people tilling it are free.

In fact, those who prize freedom only for the material benefits it offers have never kept it long.

For only in countries where it reigns can a man speak, live and breathe freely. . . . The man who asks of freedom anything other than itself is born to be a slave.

Some nations have freedom in the blood and are ready to face the greatest perils and hardships in its defense. . . . Other nations, once they have grown prosperous, lose interest in freedom and let it be snatched away from them without lifting a hand to defend it, lest they should endanger thus the comforts that, in fact, they owe to it alone. It is easy to see that what is lacking in such nations is a genuine love of freedom, that lofty aspiration which, I confess, *defies analysis. For it* [freedom's miracles] *is something one must feel and logic has no part in it.*

Charles F. Kettering, a great inventive genius, gave to freedom devotees a brilliant formula: "Nothing ever built arose to touch the skies unless some man dreamed that it should, some man believed that it could, and some man willed that it must."

Let us then believe that *the miracle of freedom will rise again!*

14

CHOOSE STATESMEN, NOT POLITICIANS

The great difference between the real statesman and the pretender is, that one sees into the future, while the other regards only the present; the one lives by the day and acts on expediency; the other acts on enduring principles and for immortality.

—EDMUND BURKE

Edmund Burke (1729–97) was born in Ireland and became a member of the British Parliament. Contrary to nearly all of its members, he was sympathetic to and promotive of the American colonies and had no hesitancy in proclaiming his position. Stalwart! He was blest with foresight, seeing into the future: America, home of the free and land of the brave! Here was found the purest practice of freedom in world history, and Burke's support was based on "enduring principles and for immortality." In my reading of history, never before or since his time has there been a greater statesman— exemplar par excellence!

Let me begin by a brief commentary on immortality. Those of us who are freedom devotees have no chance of advancing our cause unless we are consistent. And consistency is impossible unless we reason from a sound premise. There are three parts to mine:

1. Man did not create himself for it is easily demonstrable that man knows next to nothing about himself. So, my first assumption is the primacy and supremacy of what I refer to as an Infinite Consciousness.
2. While it is difficult, it is nevertheless possible for the individual to increase his or her own awareness, his or her own consciousness.
3. I cannot demonstrate this but only know it to be a truth, namely, the *immortality* of the human spirit, this earthly moment being *only the beginning*.

My dictionary makes a distinction between statesmen and politicians similar to Burke's:

Politician: a person holding or seeking political office; frequently used in a derogatory sense, with implications of seeking personal or partisan gain, scheming, opportunism, etc.; as distinguished from *statesman,* which suggests able far-seeing principled conduct of public affairs.

A few comments about pretenders—politicians—those who act on expediency, seekers of personal gain, schemers. Wrote Shakespeare: "A politician—one that would circumvent God." Of the countless know-it-alls, ever so many accuse them of "playing God." Wrong! God never lords it over us. We make or break ourselves. Excellent instruction on this point by the Scottish biographer Samuel Smiles (1812–1904): ". . . there is not an act or thought in the life of a human being but carries with it a train of consequences, the end of which we may never trace. Not one but, to a certain extent, gives color to our own life, and insensibly influences the lives of those about us. The good deed or thought will live, even though we may not see it fructify but so will the bad, and no person is so insignificant as to be sure that his example will not do good on the one hand, nor evil on the other.''

Enough of the negative—evil doers: politicians. Reflect now on the positive, those whose actions are promotive of enduring principles, as were Burke's: *statesmen*. ''Principle is a passion for truth and right.''

Wrote the English novelist Bulwer-Lytton (1803–73): ''What is the essence and the life of character? *Principle*, integrity, independence, or as one of our great old writers has it, 'That inbred loyalty unto virtue.' '' Bulwer-Lytton, being of a later generation, may have learned this from Burke. In any event, his reference to independence proves that he had foresight: independent America!

The American clergyman William E. Alger (1822–1905), gave this counsel: ''True statesmanship is the art of changing a nation from what it is to what it ought to be.''

This is sound advice for present-day Americans. Moreover, I feel certain he would agree that our country cannot remain *as is*. Nothing in nature remains identical from moment to moment; everything is in constant change. Thus, we will experience a continuing downfall into the welfare state and the planned economy—socialism—or a reversal into freedom, with everyone free to act creatively as he or she pleases. This requires a diminishing number of politicians and an increasing number of statesmen.

What is required for the achievement of such a phenomenon? First, forget about working at the political level! What then? More of us than now must strive to improve our understanding and explanations of how freedom works its miracles! If enough of us are good enough, statesmen will displace politicians at local, state and federal levels—the Burkes instead of the Hitlers.

How hopeful is our situation? The record of history gives us plenty of grounds for optimism. It has been a succession of ups and downs from the world's first civilization—the Sumerians—till the present. In England and America we have witnessed several ups and downs during the last seven decades. It has been evolution/devolution in a rhythmic sequence. These swings are remindful of a clock's pendulum: left toward socialism, right toward freedom. Our societal pendulum has swung to the left as far as it is going to go. That's my faith. May it also be yours!

The English poet and critic Samuel Coleridge (1772–1834): "The three great ends for a statesman are, security to possessors, facility to acquirers, and *liberty* and *hope* to the people."

A final thought by Charles F. Kettering: "Nothing ever built arose to touch the skies unless some man dreamed that it should, some man believed that it could, and some man willed that it must." Let us dream and believe and will that freedom for one and all is in the offing.

15

THE SOURCE OF PROGRESS

> *Change of opinion is often only the progress of sound thought and growing knowledge; and though sometimes regarded as inconsistency, it is but the noble inconsistency natural to a mind ever ready for growth and expansion of thought, and that never fears to follow where truth and duty may lead the way.*
>
> **—TRYON EDWARDS**

This theologian (1809–94) was the compiler of my favorite quotation book, entitled *The New Dictionary of Thought*. After reading the above, typical of his wisdom, one can understand why I regard him as among the all-time greats.

Change of opinion is often only the progress of sound thought and growing knowledge. This statement voices a truth that my own experience confirms. Whenever I come upon a new thought, or a bit of knowledge gained from others, or am blest with an intuitive flash, my opinions change and are improved.

Tryon Edwards has assembled ever so many quotes under "Opinion." I feel that it is my duty to share these with FEE's ideological and philosophical friends: those who also are devoted to freedom.

The American author and editor Walter Lippmann (1889–1974): "Where mass opinion dominates the government, there is a morbid derangement of the functions of power. The prevailing public opinion has been destructively wrong at the critical juncture." Lippmann lived during a period when the principles that accounted for America's greatness had almost been forgotten. Mass opinion, featured by the vicious notion of living at the expense of others, did and still does account for the morbid derangement of the true functions of government. Have a look at the ten points of the Communist Manifesto and you will be shocked at the extent to which we have approximated or adopted them.[1]

The Danish physician A. Barthelina (1597–1643) more than three centuries ago offered us a sample of the kind of thinking that would prevent the present deplorable slump toward the communistic way of life: "Security is never an absolute. The government of a free people must take certain chances for the sake of maintaining freedom which the government of a police state avoids because it holds freedom to be of no value." The truth? In the politico-economic realm it is only freedom that is valuable! Over the past fifty years I have known many socialists, communists, welfare-staters, call this ignorance what you will, who have done a complete flip-flop to the freedom way of life. How come? Brilliant explanations of how freedom works its wonders by such great thinkers as Bastiat, Weaver, Hazlitt, Rogge, and many others—for all I know, perhaps by your enlightened self!

To demonstrate the enlightenment common to great thinkers, here is another by Edwards: "He that resolves on any

---

[1] See "Ignorance: Agent of Destruction" in my book, *Vision* (The Foundation for Economic Education, Irvington, N.Y., 1978), pp. 82–88.

The Path of Duty

great and good end, has, by that very resolution, scaled the chief barrier to it. He will find such resolution removing difficulties, searching out or making means, giving courage for despondency, and strength for weakness, and like the star to the wise men of old, ever guiding him nearer and nearer to perfection.''

In the above Edwards gives us the foundation for evolution. Robert Andrews Millikan (1868–1953), a renowned physicist and a FEE Trustee in our early days, gave us the formula in more detail: ''Three ideas stand out above all others in the influence they have exerted and are destined to exert upon the development of the human race: the idea of the Golden Rule, the idea of natural law and the idea of age-long growth or evolution.''

Contemplate the idea of the Golden Rule: ''Do as you would be done by.'' The Golden Rule, variously phrased, is found in all of the world's great religions. Jesus uttered the version most familiar to us, but Confucius spoke about the same words centuries earlier. The Golden Rule is part of the heritage of humanity; it is, so to speak, a law of human nature.

Go back to the Old Testament for an account of the evolution of man's understanding of his relation to God. This is best traced in the succession of the prophets—Amos, Isaiah, Jeremiah and the others. The evolution of thought and spirit in the succession of the prophets of Israel laid the foundation for Jesus' teaching that men and women are children of God.

Jesus' teaching prepared the greatest advance in mankind's evolution in all history. His disciples—*only twelve, with one a defector*—shared His wisdom with others who, in turn, became leaders of His Truth from that day to this. What should we learn from this? Then, now and forever, the advance of Righteousness is a matter of leadership, not a numbers problem!

Ralph Waldo Emerson: "A man cannot utter two or three sentences without disclosing to intelligent ears precisely where he stands in life and thought, whether in the kingdom of the senses and the understanding or in that of ideas and imagination, or in the realm of intuitions and duty."

While I make no claim to "intelligent ears," I have time after time, in reading a single sentence by the Sage of Concord, been enlightened by his wisdom. A few samplings:

- Trust men and they will be true to you, trust them greatly and they will show greatness themselves.
- Every great and commanding movement in the annals of the world is the triumph of enthusiasm. Nothing great was ever achieved without it.
- I cannot find language of sufficient energy to convey my sense of the sacredness of integrity.
- Cause and effect, means and ends, seed and fruit, cannot be severed; for the effect already blooms in the cause, the end pre-exists in the means, the fruit in the seed.

I shall conclude with two enlightening thoughts:

Thomas Jefferson: "Error of opinion may be tolerated where reason is left free to combat it."

Goethe: "Let us not dream that reason can ever be popular. Passions, emotions, may be made popular, but reason remains ever the property of the few."

Give America a few more individuals with Jefferson's and Goethe's power to reason and America will be free!

16

SAY "YES" TO LIFE

*Believe you can do the impossible.
Try laughing when circumstances in
your life make you want to cry. Act
as if you possess the quality you feel
you lack. On a day when you feel you
have nothing to be thankful for, write
a thank-you letter to someone who
once made a difference in your life.
Open the door to enthusiastic, joyous people.*
—NORMAN VINCENT PEALE

Dr. Peale, whom I met thirty-some years ago, has just sent me his new book, *The Treasury of Joy and Enthusiasm*. He is one of the most widely-read inspirational authors of all time. Three of his outstanding books which reveal his laudable and optimistic thinking: *The Power of Positive Thinking, A Guide to Confident Living* and *You Can if You Think You Can*. In addition to his many writings and lectures, he is Pastor of New York City's Marble Collegiate Church.

Dr. Peale inspired this essay. There is no one, past or present, whose thinking I more enthusiastically share than this contemporary of mine. First and foremost is his optimism. As one sage wrote: "It will all come right in time: the great American gospel." The gospel? Unseating government as the endower of men's rights and placing the Creator there! Here are some excellent thoughts by an unknown author:

The world is not going to the dogs. The human race is not doomed. Civilization is not going to crash. The Captain is on the bridge. Humanity is going through a difficult time, but humanity has gone through difficulties many times before in its long history, and has always come through, strengthened and purified.

Do not worry yourself about the universe collapsing. It is not going to collapse, and anyway that question is none of your business. The Captain is on the bridge. If the survival of humanity depended upon you or me, it would be a poor lookout for the Great Enterprise, would it not?

The Captain is on the bridge. God is still in business. All that you have to do is to recognize the presence of God where trouble seems to be, to do your nearest duty to the very best of your ability; and to keep an even mind until the storm is over.

This is the case for optimism, as opposed to pessimism; it also is instructive as to the avoidance of know-it-all-ness. Keep an even mind until the storm—socialism—has blown itself out. Also, it is highly religious and in harmony with Dr. Peale's moral and spiritual ascendancy.

This essay will include Dr. Peale's six suggestions for living the righteous life, along with my comments.

Believe you can do the impossible. Prior to invention of the telephone, it was impossible for the human voice to be heard more than half the distance of a football field. Alexander Graham Bell believed he could do the impossible.

Result? Around the world at the speed of light: one-seventh of a second!

The storage battery impossible? It is reported that Thomas Alva Edison, the world's greatest inventive genius, made 50,000 experiments before he succeeded in producing the storage battery. He was asked after his success if he didn't get discouraged working so long without results. "Results," he exclaimed, "Why, I learned 50,000 things I didn't know before." His 50,000 problems were blessings in disguise! So are our problems.

Try laughing when circumstances in your life make you want to cry. A majority of citizens whose objective is liberty for one and all are saddened by our slump into socialism. They are forlorn and have no hope for a turnabout. "They want to cry" appropriately describes their dejection. They throw in the sponge and, by so doing, make the objective of socialists easier to attain. Such sorrow makes each day a doomsday. Wrote Sir Walter Raleigh: "Sorrows are dangerous companions, converting bad into evil and evil into worse."

Act as if you possess the quality you feel you lack. A few of us, myself included, feel that we lack the quality, the ability, adequately to explain the freedom philosophy with sufficient clarity. No one, to my knowledge, has even approached perfection in this matter. Explaining creativity at the human level borders on the difficulties everyone faces when trying to describe Creation itself. However, we must keep in mind the encouraging truth that the act of becoming is achieved by overcoming. The English critic and author William Hazlitt (1778–1830) sheds light on the value of difficulties: "Our energy is in proportion to the resistance it meets. We attempt nothing great but from a sense of the difficulties we have to encounter; we persevere in nothing great but from a pride in *overcoming* them."

The French dramatist Molière (1622–73): "The greater the obstacle, the more glory we have in overcoming it. The difficulties with which we are met are the maids of honor which set off virtue."

Edmund Burke: "Difficulty is a sense instructor set over us by the Supreme guardian and legislator who knows us better than we know ourselves and leaves us better too. He that wrestles with us strengthens our nerves and sharpens our skill. Our antagonist is our helper."

These observations about difficulties do, indeed, make it plain that they sharpen our skills to labor day in and day out on behalf of liberty!

On a day when you have nothing to be thankful for, write a thank-you letter to someone who has made a difference in your life. I cannot remember a day in my 83 years in which I have had nothing to be thankful for. Write thank-you letters to those who have made a difference in my life? Yes, to contemporaries who have helped me in my thinking. However, my greatest helpers are those who have passed to their reward, such sages as Confucius, Socrates, Edmund Burke, Frederic Bastiat, Adam Smith, Washington, Jefferson, Lincoln, Emerson, and ever so many others. No thank-you letters. What then?

I have quoted these intellectual, moral and spiritual giants over and over again in my 28 books. Also in *Notes from FEE* going to 50,000 freedom devotees. Readers, in turn, do the same among those in their orbit. Result? The wisdom of these sages I have quoted does not rest in the grave with them. Instead, it graces generation after generation.

Thanks for my opportunity to serve others, now and hereafter, by discovering and sharing truths that advance an understanding of liberty.

Open the door to enthusiastic, joyous people. Wrote
Emerson: "Every great and commanding movement in the
annals of the world is the triumph of enthusiasm. Nothing
great was ever achieved without it." Ever so many citizens
on our side are forlorn and see no hope for the future. How
wonderful it would be were they to heed the counsel of that
English poet Samuel Coleridge (1772–1834): "Enlist the
interests of stern morality and religious enthusiasm in the
cause of *political liberty,* as in the time of the old Puritans,
and it will be irresistible." It was the old Puritans and their
remarkable thinking that set the stage for the Declaration of
Independence.

I like what the English divine Robert South (1634–1716)
had to say about joyous people: "The very society of joy
redoubles it; so that, while it lights upon my friend it redoubles upon myself, and the brighter his candle burns the more
easily it will light mine."

So, let us joyfully practice freedom and say "yes" to life.

17

KINDNESS AND INTELLIGENCE

Jesus and Socrates, out of very different backgrounds, are saying the same thing. Intelligence is kindness. Kindness is intelligence. The fundamental which the two terms suggest in different ways . . . is the same quality on which all human civilization is built.
—ALEXANDER MEIKLEJOHN

This American educator (1872–1964) provides an insight which, if understood and practiced, would lead in a most admirable manner toward a return to freedom in America— the perception that civilization is based on a kindly intelligence. Civilization is achieved in "the countries and peoples considered to have reached a high stage of social and cultural development," and it requires the practice of certain human excellences.

May we say that kindness and intelligence are the two foremost virtues that lie at the root of civilization? I believe, as Meiklejohn, that they are twins and that neither fully exists without the other. Goethe exemplified intelligence and added that "*Kindness is the golden chain by which society is bound together.*"

"Jesus and Socrates, out of very different backgrounds, are saying the same thing." A few samplings:

Socrates: Do not be angry with me if I tell you the truth.
Jesus: The truth shall make you free.
Socrates: First and chiefly care about the improvement of the soul.
Jesus: What is a man profited, if he shall gain the whole world, and lose his own soul?
Socrates: No evil can beface a good man either in life or death.
Jesus: Fear not them which kill the body, but are not able to kill the soul.

These are the exemplarities which, if we devotedly follow, will lead to a rebuilding of our American civilization!

"Do not be angry with me if I tell you the truth." Well might the socialists—and any others who even minutely infract the freedom way of life—heed this Socratic admonishment. Anger is a dastardly, cowardly trait. I at least try not to get angry at my ideological opponents. I only feel sorry for know-it-alls, those in or out of politics. Why avoid anger? There are two good reasons: (1) anger hardens others in their ways and keeps them away from the freedom philosophy, and (2) anger poisons the soul of him who yields to it. Thomas Jefferson proposed a method of avoidance. "When angry, count ten before you speak; if very angry, count a hundred." Better yet, to put anger behind you, count your blessings!

"The truth shall make you free." Wrote the English novelist Bulwer-Lytton: "One of the sublimest things in the world is plain truth." What might qualify for this sublime

elevation? Living truth is the freedom to act creatively as we please! Falsehood enslaves, for, as John Dryden said, "Truth is the foundation of all knowledge and the cement of all societies." No question about it, mankind's highest elevation is *Truth*! "Truth is beautiful and divine no matter how humble its origin," said Michael Pupin.

Confirmations? "Out of the mouths of babes and sucklings hast thou ordained strength." We must never scorn a truth because of its humble origin. Recently, I received a letter from a grade school student, ten years of age, explaining the freedom philosophy far better than most of those who have the titles of teachers and preachers. As Thoreau wrote, "Humility like darkness reveals the heavenly lights." An appropriate ambition? Search for these lights from sources near and far, past and present, that we may brighten our own lights!

Reflect on the following by an author unknown to me:

Fueled by a million man-made wings of fire . . . the rocket tore through the sky . . . and everybody cheered.
Fueled only by a thought from God, the seedling urged its way through the thickness of black . . . and as it pierced the heavy ceiling of the soil . . . and launched itself into outer space . . . No one even clapped.

Fueled by a thought from God. Alexander Cruden wrote: "God. This is one of the names we give to that eternal, infinite and *incomprehensible* being, the creator of all things, who preserves and governs everything by his almighty power and wisdom, and who is the only object of our worship."

I would amend the above by changing "is" to "should"— "who *should* be the only object of our worship." Only atheists would dispute this. Hear this by John Foster: "The atheist is one of the most daring beings in creation, a contemner [scorner] who explodes his laws by denying his existence." I am acquainted with many who embrace atheism, and I regard such a position as incompatible with the freedom philosophy.

"The greatest homage we can pay to truth is to use it," said Emerson. There are ever so many individuals who know freedom works its miracles. But how many use this truth in conversations, speeches and writings? Only a few! Why? The fear of unpopularity; thus silence.

Let me conclude this little essay with a brilliant thought by the American poet, William Cullen Bryant (1794–1878):

> Truth, crushed to earth, shall rise again—
> The eternal years of God are hers:
> But Error, wounded, writhes in pain,
> And dies among his worshipers.

Here we have a truth which all history confirms, namely, the rise and fall of nations. Bryant, during his life span, observed the greatest societal ascent of all time: our United States of America! He passed to his reward two decades before the beginning of our decline into the welfare state and the planned economy.

Bryant, however, was prescient. He knew that truth will rise again, and it was this wisdom that accounted for his optimism, foreseeing the turnabout that is presently beginning. Past error does, indeed, writhe in pain and will die, as will the dictatorial thinking of its socialistic worshipers.

In the practice of kindness and intelligence lies our hope for rebuilding a civilized America.

18

SUBLIME EXAMPLE

Lives of great men all remind us
We can make our lives sublime.
And, departing, leave behind us
Footprints on the sands of time.
—H. W. LONGFELLOW

The meaning of "sublime"? It is "elevated, exalted, lofty, superb." Those who attain this status are, indeed, examples of righteousness; they are individuals, past and present, who attract others to intellectual, moral and spiritual growth. As Edmund Burke wrote, "Example is the school of mankind. They will learn at no other." If we would make our lives sublime—freedom of everyone to act creatively as each pleases—we would strive to become exemplars in the school of mankind, as did our Founding Fathers. If we succeed, we too would leave behind us "footprints on the sands of time." The following is what several wise men have had to say about the importance of exemplarity.

The German philosopher Immanuel Kant (1724–1804): "So act that your principle of action might safely be made a law for the whole world." How may you or I act so that our principle of action *might* safely be made a law for the whole world? This philosopher used the word, "might," which attests to his wisdom. The very best any of us can do is to approximate the Infinite Unknown. The appropriate method? To *draw* on the greatest thinkers of all time, Kant being one of them!

The American author and editor Christian Bovee (1820–1904): "Example has more followers than reason. We unconsciously imitate what pleases us and approximate to the characters we most admire. A generous habit of thought and action carries with it an incalculable influence." Were there no means of advancement in thought and action beyond the solitary individual's ability to reason, there would be little if any growth in consciousness or an awareness of what things are good—the free market being high on any intelligent listing of mankind's blessings. What to do? Seek light from those more enlightened than self, Bovee being another one of ever so many examples! To the extent that we progress in thought and action, to that extent are others attracted by our example—the law of attraction!

The English poet, dramatist and novelist Oliver Goldsmith (1728–74): "People seldom improve when they have no better model than themselves to copy after." The synonym for "model," according to my dictionary, implies "flawless, ideal, perfect." To "copy after" means to imitate. Who, then, should we copy after? Jesus ranks first! Who else? Any person whose competence is above one's own. Diligent search will reveal countless exemplars who can bless our lives!

The Greek historian Herodotus (484–425 B.C.): "I am satisfied that we are less convinced by what we hear than by what we see." The word "see" has ever so many meanings, ranging from what can be seen by the eyes to what can be discovered, learned, perceived. While I have no proof, it seems certain that this wise Greek used "see" in the latter sense.

Less convinced by what we hear. In his time there were no newspapers. No one even dreamed of a telephone, radio or TV. Herodotus heard little more from others than what his unlearned neighbors had to say. There were some other outstanding scholars in Greece in those days, but little opportunity for close contact between them. "Learning makes a man fit company for himself." So, it seems that Herodotus was largely self-taught.

Now to our time. What do we hear? With some notable exceptions, nothing but bad news. Citizens by the millions are imitators and thus see nothing wrong in such chicanery. This despicable be-like-me-ness is not limited to murder, theft, rape and other such sins. It is to be noted in numerous walks of life. For a single example, corporations inhibiting free trade, getting government to bail them out of bankruptcy, on and on. No more than Herodotus should any of us be satisfied with the folderol we hear!

Suppose Herodotus could see what has happened in the world since his time. A veritable explosion in creativity, especially in the U.S.A. In spite of the growing socialism, freedom to produce and exchange surpasses that of any other nation. In reacting against socialistic error, an increasing number of Americans are seeking and learning the truth of freedom—exemplars! And for that response, I am grateful.

The English poet Edmund Spenser (1552–99): "Much more gracious and profitable is doctrine by example than by rule." He wrote the above when mercantilism was the rule of his country: "Ownership and control of the means of production and distribution by the people as a whole." The meaning of "people as a whole"? Collectivism, the welfare state and the planned economy, a coercive rejection of the rights of individuals to act creatively as they please, of their freedom to produce and exchange voluntarily.

Much more gracious and profitable is doctrine by example. Time and again I have claimed that ours is not a numbers problem. An interesting reflection on this point by San Pedro of Alcantara:

> May your Lordship not torment yourself: there is a remedy for this deluge of crimes. Let us be, you and me, that which we should be. There will be two less souls to convert. Let each person behave thus; it is the most efficacious of reforms. The trouble is that no one wants to correct himself and everyone meddles at correcting others, thus everything stays as is.

I would modify that last sentence to read, "nearly everyone." In our day there are thousands in the U.S.A. and other nations who are concentrating on self-improvement so that they may become exemplars of the freedom philosophy.

19

EARNEST RESOLUTION

To think we are able is almost to be so; to determine upon attainment is frequently attainment itself; earnest resolution has often seemed to have about it almost a savor of omnipotence. —**SAMUEL SMILES**

Suppose we were to understand and adhere to the above by this English biographer (1812–1904). How could we phrase the result? Earnest resolution would lead to a revolution, that is, to a turnabout from the socialistic road we have been on for the past eight decades to the way of life Americans earlier enjoyed: the freedom way of life—blessings galore!

Several reflections on blessings. "Nothing raises the price of blessing like its removal; whereas it was its continuance which should have taught us its value." The English author Izaak Walton (1593–1683), gives support to this excellent thought: "Blessings we enjoy daily, and for the most of them, and because they be so common, men forget to pay their praises. . . . Let me tell you that every misery I miss is a new blessing."

Nothing raises the price of blessing like its removal. Why this high price? Because we never know the value of our blessings until lost. By nature man is fallible. Never being able to know much—regardless of how much knowledge is acquired—is a built-in condition of the human species. Escaping from ignorance, that is, progressing everlastingly, is an everlasting process.

To grow in harmony with Infinite Consciousness is a goal toward which man can ever strive but never attain. Any individual, aware of his natural ignorance, will readily realize that the more he knows the more will he expose himself to the unknown. As his stock of knowledge expands, the more conscious will he be of how much more there is beyond his ken. But by knowing something, however little, man does ascend and improve his situation; in an infinitesimal way, he thus participates in Creation. Viewed broadly enough, this appears to be human destiny. In any event, moving from the depths of ignorance to lesser ignorance is a process favorable to the unobstructed flow of creativities: the free market.

I repeat, ignorance of itself is not the enemy of the free and unfettered market. Ignorance is universal among humans. Were sheer ignorance the culprit, there never would have been any freedom in the market, none whatsoever. The real foe is *ignorance of being ignorant;* ignorance of the fact that man in his earthly station is limited at best to a growth in knowledge. Any person not in this state of awareness is, perforce, a know-it-all. These poor souls are unaware of their countless blessings. Removal! And what a high price this vacuity—going through life in a state of mental emptiness!

Let me tell you that every misery I miss is a new blessing. Why did Izaak Walton refer to the missing of a misery as a new blessing? I shall hazard a guess. He, unlike most individuals, was aware of blessings that grace the lives of everyone. To him, they were countless, common and, therefore, taken for granted. Freedom to act creatively as one pleases, every heart beat, all sorts of intellectual and moral and spiritual improvement, everything that gives happiness and prevents misfortune are but an infinitesimal fraction of our blessings. How few there are who count them or even think of doing so!

Every misery one misses is, indeed, a *new* blessing. Misery? According to the dictionary: "unhappiness, woe, wretchedness, agony, poverty, despondency, grief, sorrow."

The missing of these miseries is a blessing in disguise. It is overcoming them—resulting in their absence—that makes them a *new blessing!* This by an unknown: "The nerve which never relaxes—the eye which never blanches—the thought which never wanders—the purpose that never wavers—these are the masters of victory." This individual, I suspect, had the freedom way of life in mind. In any event, he or she presented the virtues that are necessary for a politico-economic turnabout, a resurgence of freedom.

The purpose that never wavers was brilliantly emphasized by the English minister William Punshon (1824–81): "It is the old lesson—a worthy purpose, patient energy for its accomplishment, a resoluteness undaunted by difficulties, and then success."

Our Founding Fathers had a *worthy purpose,* unmatched in all history, ". . . unalienable Rights, . . . among them . . . Life, Liberty and the pursuit of Happiness." They did, indeed, have a patient energy for accomplishing their purposes and a resoluteness undaunted by difficulties. Success? Never before or since has there been such a remarkable achievement: self-responsibility and all citizens free to act creatively as they please. Result? The greatest outburst of prosperity and the good life ever known!

True, the roots of this civilized explosion are forgotten by most citizens and we Americans *have been* suffering the penalty. Happily, a turnabout seems possible in the near future. Let each of us do his part in bringing about the coming victory. Nothing is more joyful than ardent participation!

Smiles was right in asserting that "earnest resolution has often seemed to have about it a savor of omnipotence." Being a first-rate freedom devotee, he meant that creativity at the human level savored of Creation—the Heavenly Level. Those persons so graced are on their way to life's *Highest Purpose*.

The nature of our purpose or task is indicated by the famed economist F. A. Hayek:

> We at least believe that we have attained an understanding of the forces which have shaped civilization which our opponents lack. Yet, if we have not convinced them, the reason must be that we have not yet made explicit some of the foundations on which our conclusions rest. Our chief task, therefore, must still be to improve the argument on which our case for a free society rests.

Wrote Christina, Queen of Sweden (1626–89): "It is necessary to try to surpass one's self always; this occupation ought to last as long as life." Perpetual self-improvement and an understanding and explanation of freedom should be the earnest resolution of each of us.

20

ATTRACTION

If a man can write a better book, preach a better sermon, or make a better mouse-trap than his neighbor, though he build his home in the woods, the world will make a beaten path to his door.

The above is generally attributed to Emerson (1808–82) but Elbert Hubbard (1859–1915) claimed it was his. Were I 130 years younger, I would claim it as mine, for I have been citing this same law of attraction for nearly 50 years.

Anthony Standen of this century, a famous scientist, emphasized the same basic idea in the following which I have used over and over again:

All the phenomena of astronomy, which had baffled the acutest minds since the dawn of history, the movement of the heavens, of the sun and the moon, the very complex movement of the planets, suddenly tumble together and become intelligible in terms of the one staggering assumption, this *mysterious "attractive force."* And not only the movement of the heavenly bodies, far more than that, the movement of earthly bodies too are seen to be subject to the same mathematically definable law, instead of being, as they were for all previous philosophers, mere unpredictable happen-so's.

Standen may not have had human beings in mind when he referred to "earthly bodies," but the principle of attraction applies across the boards, to physical nature and especially to human nature. Applied to humanity, this "mysterious attractive force" works in all cases of personal advancement.

With the law of attraction as a working premise, it is interesting to observe what people have had to say about the attainment of success. A few see dangers in succeeding, others applaud the determination to achieve. Here are two samplings that warn of the danger. An American clergyman, Henry Ward Beecher (1813–87): "Success is full of promise till men get it, and then it is as a last year's nest from which the bird has flown."

The nonconformist English divine Ralph Venning (1620–73): "Success at first doth many times undo men at last."

Ever so many people, in every walk of life, once they excel others in their respective fields, "think" they have it made and slump into do-nothings. They glory *only* in their past achievements, rest on their laurels—life's mission at an end. Success undoes them, resulting in an entrepreneurial death! Wrote one sage: "It is not death, it is dying that alarms me."

However, many wise men see only good in striving to succeed. The American journalist and poet Edgar A. Guest can be counted among them:

> Somebody said that it couldn't be done,
> But he with a chuckle replied
> That "maybe it couldn't," but he would be one
> Who wouldn't say so till he'd tried.

Reflect on the things that couldn't be done by Cro-Magnon men, 35,000 years ago. They had no pens or pencils with which to write, nor did they have anything in their minds worth writing about. No need to comment on the wonders that have taken place in the meantime: man evolving intellectually, morally, spiritually. What else? A prosperity that would have stunned these ancients, that is, if their "minds" were capable of such comprehension!

Edgar Guest grasped the genesis of progress, that virtue which sparks the road to freedom. Determination to succeed is indeed a virtue. If we do not move forward in any category of life we condemn ourselves to slipping backward.

The road to success is marked by individuals who with a chuckle admit the difficulty but determine to try. Observe how often such individuals with this drive succeed. They lay the steppingstones to progress—and find joy in the effort.

According to the famous actress Marie Dressler: "Never one thing and seldom one person can make for a success. It takes a number of them merging into one perfect whole."

As I have written many times, it's tiny bits of expertise by the countless millions, freely flowing, configurating and "merging"—that wend their way to prosperity. One never knows from whom the light will shine. The lesson? Always be on the lookout!

Wrote the great scientist Albert Einstein (1879–1955): "A successful man is he who receives a great deal more from his fellowmen, usually incomparably more, than corresponds to his service to them." What a truism! Einstein set forth the theory of relativity in 1905. He received the Nobel prize for physics in 1921. Greatness made no egotist of this genius. The above attests to his humility, the absence of pride.

In a country where the citizens are as free as Americans and their talents are as diversified as ours, not one could exist on his or her endeavors. *We are interdependent*! Einstein could not exist on physics any more than I can on writing or you on your specialization. Starvation! In our stage of advancement, each of us does, indeed, receive *incomparably* more from others than they receive from any one of us. A doff of the hat to the millions who serve each of us!

An interesting thought by the English author Charles Buxton (1823–71): "The road to success is not to be run upon by seven-leagued boots. Step by step, little by little, bit by bit—that is the way to wealth, that is the way to wisdom, that is the way to glory, pounds are the sons not of pounds, but of pence."

Seldom, if ever, does one attain wealth or wisdom in one stride. At best, it is bit by bit, step by step—the glorious road to freedom!

There is joy in attaining so great a power of attraction to the freedom way of life that others will make *a beaten path to our door*!

21

A BENEFACTOR TO MANKIND

The greatest and most inoffensive path of life leads through the avenues of science and learning; and whoever can remove any obstruction in this way, or open up any new prospect, ought, so far, to be esteemed a benefactor to mankind.

—DAVID HUME

This Scottish historian and philosopher (1711–1776) was a close friend of Adam Smith. His *History of England* became famous; likewise his philosophical works. Hume was considered a skeptic, but skepticism was most appropriate prior to the overthrow of mercantilism. It is more than likely that Hume's ideas helped to shape Adam Smith's great book, *The Wealth of Nations,* which in turn proved enlightening and useful to our Founding Fathers.

Goethe, a German, born a half century later than Hume, also gave to posterity high-grade goals, which if pursued would assure a good society. Equally important, Goethe offered a workable methodology:

He who wishes to exert a useful influence must be careful to insult nothing. Let him not be troubled by what seems absurd, but concentrate his energies to the creation of what is good. He must not demolish, but build. He must raise temples where mankind can come and partake of the purest pleasures.

It appears that the objectives Hume and Goethe had in mind are similar to FEE's goals. And our methodology appears to be the same, namely, emphasize learning and the good as the way to freedom.

Plato, the Greek philosopher (427–347 B.C.), warned that "The learning and knowledge we have is, at the most, but little compared with that of which we are ignorant." There is no individual, past or present, who understands and can explain Creation at the Heavenly level. And I am unaware of anyone who has more than a tiny inkling of how creation at the human level works its miracles. No earthling, regardless of his or her genius, knows how to make a pencil. Simple? Unbelievably complex! Plato grasped this point twenty-four centuries ago.

The English critic and author William Hazlitt (1778–1830) discovered that: "The most learned are often the most narrow-minded men." Hazlitt was obviously referring to those who are puffed up with pride by reason of their academic titles, their Ph.D.'s and other labels related to schooling. They "think" they have no more to learn, and such pride is, indeed, narrow-minded. "Pride goeth before destruction, and a haughty spirit before a fall." Proverbs 16:18.

Sir John Powell, seventeenth-century English jurist, advised: "He who has no inclination to learn more will be very apt to think he knows enough." Some have no inclination to learn more about freedom. In their blindness they assume that they know enough already. And the result is that they become copycats of socialists, past and present.

The American philosopher Ralph Barton Perry (1876–1957): "Ignorance deprives men of freedom because they do not know what alternatives there are. It is impossible to choose what one has never 'heard of.' "

Ignorance does, indeed, deprive men of knowing what freedom is; and so they lapse into freedom's opposite, socialism! Why do they give in to this despicable way of life? Although they may have "heard of" freedom, the reality is beyond their understanding. Wrote the English essayist Sir Richard Steele (1672–1729): "I know no evil so great as the abuse of the understanding and there is no one vice more common." Let us make the failure to understand freedom less common by perfecting our own understanding of it.

Confucius, Chinese moral teacher and sage, is my oldest mentor, doing his excellent thinking about 2,500 years ago. Several samplings of his thinking follow:

- Learning without thought is useless. Thought without learning is dangerous.
- Not to enlighten one who can be enlightened, is to waste a man, to endeavor to enlighten one who cannot be enlightened is to waste words. The intelligent man wastes neither his man nor his words.
- To see what is right and not do it is a want of courage.

Those who are courageous enough to do no wrong will find confirmation in the following words of wisdom.

True courage is not the brutal force of vulgar heroes, but the firm resolve of virtue and reason. *—Paul Whitehead*

A great deal of talent is lost in the world for its want of a little courage.   —*Sydney Smith*

A coward flows backward away from new things. A man of courage flows forward, in the midst of new things.
               —*Jacques Maritain*

A concluding thought by Confucius: "I will not be concerned by other men not knowing me; I will be concerned at my own want of ability." And the thought has been elaborated by the American author Elbert Hubbard (1859–1915): "There is something much more scarce, something finer far, something rarer than ability. It is the ability to recognize ability."

It does not concern me that I am not known to the multitudes. Not one person in a million ever heard of me or ever will. The fact is irrelevant, for those of us devoted to the freedom way of life and its return recognize that ours is not a numbers problem. What then? Edmund Burke gave us the answer: "Example is the school of mankind; they will learn at no other." The German philosopher, Immanuel Kant (1724–1804) pointed to that high level of exemplarity at which we should strive: "So act that your principle of action might safely be made a law for the whole world."

How may we become benefactors to mankind? Learn and consistently abide by guidelines such as these:

- Ours is not a selling but a learning problem.
- Realize how little we know and seek the wisdom of sages past and present.
- Never disparage our socialistic opponents but, instead, demonstrate the fallacy of socialistic notions.
- Never, under any circumstance, permit any "leaks" or "buts."
- Stand ramrod straight for freedom!

22

GOVERN THYSELF

Society cannot exist unless a controlling power upon will and appetite be placed somewhere; and the less of it there is within, the more there must be without. It is ordained in the eternal constitution of things, that men of intemperate minds cannot be free. Their passions forge their fetters. **—EDMUND BURKE**

"Controlling power upon will and appetite must be placed somewhere." If this power be not placed aright, it is obvious that we cannot be free. If it be placed without, we will suffer all-out government, a trend that now bedevils us. On what does a reversal depend? Self-government, self-control; briefly, govern thyself.

Goethe gave his support to this truth: "What is the best government? That which teaches us to govern ourselves."

The Greek philosopher Pythagoras: "No man is free who cannot command himself."

The Roman Stoic philosopher Seneca: "Most powerful is he who has himself in his own power."

Let's begin by observing and commenting upon what several Presidents of the U.S.A. have written about the functions of government:

George Washington:

If to please the people, we offer what we ourselves disapprove, how can we afterwards defend our work? Let us raise a standard to which the wise and honest can repair. The event is in the hand of God.

Millions of citizens and politicians, for no more than the shameful ambition of gaining fortune at the expense of others, do that which if imposed on them they would disapprove. Can they afterward defend such political plundering? No more than they could defend common thievery! Consider just three among thousands of examples of political privilege:

1—Food stamps.
2—Tariffs sponsored by business firms seeking a noncompetitive status.
3—Subsidies to peanut farmers and tobacco growers.

The role of freedom devotees? Strive for that excellence in understanding and explanation which is in harmony with this Creation of which we are a part.

Abraham Lincoln:

This nation, under God, shall have a new birth of freedom, that government of the people, by the people, and for the people shall not perish from the earth.

A truth I have cited many times, by the eminent psychologist Fritz Kunkel: "Immense hidden powers lurk in the unconscious of the most common man—indeed, in all people without exception." I am unaware of any individual, past or present, in which this truth was better exemplified than in Honest Abe. Born in poverty, and of formal schooling he had almost none. Yet, so avid was he for learning that he schooled himself.

This President knew as well as anyone of freedom's birth in America. However, the greatest error of our Founding Fathers was to allow slavery. Why? They wished to bring the southern slave states into the original union with the northern non-slave states. What Lincoln meant by "a new birth of freedom" was an America without slavery. He won!

Have we a lesson to learn from his victory? For the past ten decades we have been slumping, not into a Simon Legree form of slavery but into a Marxian form: "From each according to his ability, to each according to his need."[1] What should our ambition be? The same as Lincoln's: achieve a new birth of freedom by people—you and me—that we shall not perish. Let us bring out our hidden powers.

Grover Cleveland:

Though the people support the government, the government should not support the people.

A government for the people must depend for its success on the intelligence, the morality, the justice, and the interest of the people themselves.

What a truth: "government should not support the people." Cleveland's wisdom on this point came in one of his veto messages. Congress had voted a $10,000 grant—a mere

---

[1] See "Ignorance: Agent of Destruction" in my book, *Vision* (Irvington, N.Y.: The Foundation for Economic Education, Inc., 1978), pp. 82–88.

pittance—to Texas farmers whose farms had become temporary deserts. Cleveland vetoed the proposal.

Suppose all Presidents and a majority in Congress were to believe and act as did Cleveland. We would enjoy limited government in its pristine purity! On what does such an attainment depend? He gave us the answer: "On the intelligence, the morality, the justice and the interest of the people."

It is an observed fact that whatever shows forth on the political horizon is but a reflection of whatever the preponderant thinking of the citizens happens to be. Let every one of us follow Cleveland's thinking on this point and we shall enjoy a properly limited government, all of us free to act creatively as we please!

Woodrow Wilson:

No man ever saw the people of whom he forms a part. No man ever saw a government. I live in the midst of the Government of the United States, but I never saw the Government of the United States.

I am a part of my country's people, but I have not seen, and never will see, more than a tiny fraction of them. And no more than a fraction of the population will ever see me. This is nothing to lament. "People" and "government" are abstractions, mental constructs; only individual persons are real.

I, along with President Wilson, have no more seen a government than I have seen a black cat in a dark room. Is this kind of "blindness" to be deplored? Of course not! Let each individual light his or her own candle. Seek the light of freedom in individual action!

Calvin Coolidge:

Governments are necessarily continuing concerns. They have to keep going in good times and in bad. They therefore need a wide margin of safety. If taxes and debt are made all the people can bear when times are good, there will be certain disaster when times are bad.

Properly limited government is an absolute necessity for human progress. All governments, however, are, without question, agencies that require a scrupulous attention by the citizens. Our Founding Fathers were concerned to preserve their free way of life and to avoid tyrannous forms of rule that had featured the historical past. They found it!

Our Founding Fathers wrote the greatest political document of all time, the Constitution. Unfortunately, they made several disastrous errors such as government coinage, government mail delivery and tariffs. They failed to do away with Simon Legree slavery in the South; and they supported government education.

Let us strive for and hopefully attain this glorious situation: government at all levels—federal, state and local—securing justice for one and all and keeping the peace. When the law protects life, liberty and property, there is no longer any obstacle thwarting the release of creative human energy. What would be the result? The greatest outburst of individual creativity in history—genuine well-being for you, me, and all others.

Taxes and debts are growing so rapidly that their burden far exceeds what ever so many citizens can bear. Politically manufactured poverty! These times may, for some of us, still be good, but if the present trend continues it will, as

President Coolidge wrote, "be certain disaster for everyone."

Let us share in the wisdom of Edmund Burke: "No government ought to exist for the purpose of checking the prosperity of its people or to allow such a principle in its policy." Then we may share the faith of President Lincoln: "This nation, under God, shall have a new birth of freedom."

23

THERE IS TIME ENOUGH

If time be of all things the most precious, wasting time must be the greatest prodigality, since lost time is never found again; and what we call time enough always proves little enough. Let us then be up and doing, and doing to the purpose; so by diligence shall we do more with less perplexity.

—BENJAMIN FRANKLIN

Wisdom of a high order flowed from Benjamin Franklin (1706–90), a statesman, inventor, author and a signer of The Declaration of Independence. He was a devotee of freedom whom each of us should try to emulate.

Franklin, as much as anyone, gave birth to the American miracle: a government strictly limited to keeping the peace and invoking a common justice, with everyone free to act creatively as he or she pleases. The above quotation leads us to reflect on the question: Do we or do we not have time enough? The answers are greatly varied, ranging from brilliant to depressing.

I begin with some samplings of the latter, prior to testimony from the brilliant. It is joyful to present the brilliant last in order to demonstrate where lies our hope for the future. On the depressing side, here is Demetrius, a character from Shakespeare: "Time makes all things worse."

Time does, indeed, darken the lives of millions. Lacking any aspirations to enlighten themselves, their potentialities lie dormant. These are people content to live off others. They depend on others for the creative ideas that make their existence possible, and also get food stamps, social security and ever so many other governmental hand-outs. The longer they live the more life worsens for them.

Without identifying the authors, here are a few more examples of the depressing:

Time cuts down all.

Time is the slave of error.

Time was made for slaves.

Learned man is an idler who kills time by study.

Surest poison is time.

Let us turn then to a more optimistic view of time. According to the American journalist Arthur Brisbane (1864–1936): "Regret for time wasted can become a power for good in the time that remains. And the time that remains is time enough, if we will only stop the waste and the idle, useless regretting."

Whatever one's aim in life and his level of achievement—be it success or failure, win or lose—never regret. Reflect on the millions who fail to get their chores into the past tense. Result? All is dismal, no hope! This is not only a mental sickness but an impediment to human progress. The road to success? A recognition of one's countless blessings and the knowledge that there is time enough for individual ascendancy on the part of youngsters and adults alike. Keep always in mind this truism: One does not *grow* old: one *becomes* old by not growing!

Caleb C. Colton, English clergyman (1780–1832): "Much can be done in those little shreds and patches of time, which every day produces, and which most men throw away, but which nevertheless will make at the end of it no small deduction from the life of man." Ever so many individuals have one or more good ideas daily. But ideas, as intuitive flashes, are like dreams—evanescent, fleeting, gone with the wind, as we say.

What must one do to avoid this intellectual calamity? Put it in writing; record every idea on paper the moment of reception! This is one of the reasons I have kept a daily journal for more than thirty years. Name a politico-economic thinker superior to one of FEE's founders, Henry Hazlitt. He taught me this method years ago. Emulate him for intellectual progress!

Joseph Parker, English divine (1830–1902): "Our yesterdays follow us; they constitute our life, and they give character and force and meaning to our present deeds." Live each day well, for today is tomorrow's yesterday and yesterday's tomorrow. Thus, if we would give character and force to the days and years ahead, we must concentrate on perfecting our character. When the late J. Pierpont Morgan (1837–1913), famous banker, was asked what he considered the best bank collateral, he replied, "Character." Were I a banker and had the choice of an individual with high undeviating character or present-day government bonds as collateral, which would I take? The answer is obvious!

The American statesman Robert C. Winthrop (1809–94): "The greatest contribution which any man can make for the benefit of posterity, is that of good character. The richest bequest which any man can leave to the youth of his native land, is that of a shining, spotless example." Let each of us improve our own character to the point where we are first-rate exemplars of freedom for one and all!

I shall conclude with another wise observation by Benjamin Franklin: "Does thou love life? Then do not squander time, for that is the stuff life is made of."

24

SWEET LAND OF LIBERTY

Let our object be our country, our whole country, and nothing but our country. And, by the blessing of God, may that country itself become a vast and splendid monument, not of oppression and terror, but of wisdom, of peace, and of liberty, upon which the world may gaze with admiration forever.

—DANIEL WEBSTER

This American author and statesman (1782–1852) gained the reputation of being the greatest orator of his time. Among his many attainments, he served in the House of Representatives, later in the Senate, and later on as Secretary of State. His wisdom is worthy of our serious reflections.

May America become "a vast and splendid monument" for the peoples of the world, including those of our nation today; and may future generations forever gaze upon it as representing the most remarkable achievement in all history, namely, the politico-economic structure created by our Founding Fathers. Let us also hope that Americans and those in other countries will not look upon the world's slump toward socialism as a model to emulate.

Socialism is featured by many kinds of "oppression." Two samples: (1) the squelching of citizens' desire to act creatively as they please, as for instance, the law forbidding the private delivery of first-class mail; and (2) the fantastic domination of everyone by political know-it-alls, that is, those who know not how to run their own lives but "know" how to run the lives of the entire citizenry!

With regard to monuments, hear the French novelist Joseph Joubert (1754–1824): "Monuments are the grappling-irons that bind one generation to another." Concerning the freedom way of life: the depth of our understanding and the clarity of our explanation will either bloom in the next generation, or freedom will fade. Let us strive now for that excellence which will cause future generations to bloom!

The English critic and author William Hazlitt (1778–1830), observed: "They only deserve a monument who do not need one; that is, who have raised themselves a monument in the minds and memories of men." An outstanding freedom mentor of our day, Henry Hazlitt, a descendant of William Hazlitt, might be considered a monument. How come? He seeks wisdom from his long-ago relative, and ever so many other sages over the centuries. Henry, as his forebear, William, is a monument to thousands in this and other countries.

Calvin Coolidge, a statesman and a monument in the political realm, advised us: "Patriotism is easy to understand in America. It means looking out for yourself by looking out for your country." There is no way to look out for our country except to look out for one's self—Self-improvement today and continuing through all of our tomorrows!

Said Senator Carl Schurz in a speech before the Senate in 1872:

> Our country right or wrong!
> When right to be kept right;
> When wrong to be put right!

Only a patriot could make such a pronouncement. For a century prior to that speech our country ranked high in the scale of politico-economic righteousness, that is, more so than any other past or present. But then began a decline toward socialism, the authoritarian way of life. Your role and mine? Put our country right!

Daniel Webster believed in: "Liberty and union, now and forever, one and inseparable." John Dickinson (1732–1808), confirmed the idea: "By union we stand; by dividing we fall." These two statesmen of an earlier day had thoughts in accord with Schurz's wisdom: "When wrong to be put right." Let our tactics harmonize with their rightness!

The American lawyer Emery A. Storrs (1835–85) said that: "Love of country is one of the loftiest virtues; and so treason against it has been considered among the most damning of sins." My love for my country accounts for one of my highest aspirations, namely, trying constantly to better understand and explain the freedom philosophy.

Treason against one's country is, indeed, "among the most damning of sins." And what greater treason than to subject one's country to the ravages of socialism! Let us free our country of the fallacies of coercive collectivism.

Benjamin Disraeli, English statesman and author (1804–81), added that: "Patriotism depends as much on mutual suffering as on mutual success, and it is by that experience of all fortunes and all feelings that a great national character is created.'' Those of us who believe in liberty suffer as we observe and experience present-day trends in the direction of all-out statism. Is our suffering to be lamented? To the contrary, it stimulates us to expose the fallacies of socialism and to explain why everyone should be free to act creatively as he or she pleases!

Longfellow realized that politico-economic predicaments, socialism being one of many, stimulate, at least in thoughtful individuals, an intellectual strength to overcome: ''Know how sublime a thing is to suffer and be strong.'' And Gamaliel Bailey, American journalist (1807–59), added this thought: ''Night brings out stars as sorrow shows us truth.'' Patriotism, when viewed aright, accounts for numerous high characters, those devoted to liberty for one and all!

Let us conclude with this patriotic verse by Samuel Smith (1808–95), a Baptist clergyman and author of our national hymn, ''America'':

> My country, 'tis of thee,
> Sweet land of liberty,
>   Of thee I sing.

25

TO ASPIRE AFTER VIRTUE

There is but one pursuit in life which it is in the power of all to follow, and of all to attain. It is subject to no disappointments, since he that perseveres makes every difficulty an advancement, and every conquest a victory; and this is the pursuit of virtue. Sincerely to aspire after virtue is to gain her; and zealously to labor after her ways is to receive them.
—CALEB C. COLTON

This English clergyman (1780–1832), in the above, has made an observation that deserves a great deal of careful reflection. Virtue? The dictionary defines it as "goodness, morality, righteousness."

What might be the highest goal for one who aspires to virtue? The English economist John Stuart Mill (1806–73) gave the best answer known to me: "It would not be easy, even for an unbeliever, to find a better translation of the rule of virtue from the abstract to the concrete, than to endeavor so to live that Christ would approve our life." Attainable? No, it is not, but it is the road to virtue!

There would be no road to virtue for any individual not blest with its components: integrity, honor, honesty, humility, teachableness, awe, that is, a sense of wonder before the mystery of Creation. Wrote Shakespeare: "There are more things in Heaven and earth than are dreamed of in your philosophy." The virtuous individual has the humility that graced The Bard of Avon: he realized that freedom at the human level is also couched in mystery. The importance of this realization? Evolution replaces devolution, spawned by know-it-all-ness, the greatest plague to progress.

William Penn (1644–1718), English Quaker, American colonist and founder of Pennsylvania, made this vital distinction: "To be innocent is to be not guilty; but to be virtuous is to overcome our evil feelings and intentions." Citizens by the millions are guilty and more or less innocently. Example: They partake in governmental handouts coercively derived from income honestly acquired—food stamps being but a fraction of such legal thievery. However, their innocence relieves them from *feeling* guilty. But it is possible for those poor souls to overcome their naivete by discovering their potentialities.

The explanation as to why so many rot on the vine, as we say—life's mission at an end—is that they fail to recognize an undeniable truth so well expressed by the eminent psychologist Fritz Kunkel: "*Immense hidden powers* lurk in the unconscious of the most common man, indeed, of all people without exception."

Laurence Sterne (1713–68), English clergyman and novelist, explained: "A great deal of virtue, at least the outward appearance of it, is not so much from any fixed principle, as the terror of what the world will say and the liberty it will take upon the occasion we shall give."

There are many individuals who are virtuous, as this relates to their belief in the Truth of freedom. But will they speak or write this Truth as they comprehend it? So at odds is this Truth with popular jargon, a growing belief in socialism, that their witness is scorned. Scorn they fear and they remain silent: intellectual cowards! And as Shakespeare said: "Cowards die many times before their death; the valiant die but once." These intellectual infants, doubtless unknowingly, join freedom's opponents, and liberty is denigrated!

According to the French mathematician and philosopher Blaise Pascal (1623–62): "The virtue of a man ought to be measured not by his extraordinary exertions but by his everyday conduct."

In my case, I do not employ "extraordinary exertion" as I strive for an understanding and explanation of the freedom philosophy. Instead, my work is one of my countless joys and blessings—my number one desire. Wrote Saint Augustine: "Blessedness consists in the accomplishment of our desires and in having only regular desires." My desire, as set forth above, is regular—day in and day out.

Caleb Colton added this truth: "He that is good will infallibly become better, and he that is bad will as certainly become worse, for vice, virtue and time are three that never stand still."

Become better? 'Tis intellectual, moral and spiritual progress. The Sumerians of 4,500 years ago had the problem of a nonproductive desert. A few good thinkers discovered the way to fertility and the first civilization. Later, some political know-it-alls turned the wonderful evolution into a lamentable devolution.

England is another example. For several centuries—until about 150 years ago—mercantilism, no less authoritarian than serfdom, feudalism or communism, stifled the masses. Result? Creativity was more or less dormant—deadened!

However, the ideas of that great thinker Adam Smith were beginning to bear fruit through such spokesmen as John Bright and Richard Cobden, assisted by the counsel of Frederic Bastiat. They explained not only the fallacy of mercantilism but the truth of that great principle: *freedom in transactions.* Result? Evolution—prosperity for the masses. Later, devolution. Have a look at England today.

The above are only two of ever so many evolutionary/ devolutionary sequences. The U.S.A. has experienced a similar rise and decline. We were a leader among nations for about a century. And then the holocaust, a slump into more and more socialism.

Thank Heaven that vice, virtue and time never stand still. We should and will use our time to acquire the virtue which will result in evolution.

Another good thought by Colton: "Power will intoxicate the best hearts, as wine the strongest heads. No man is wise enough to be trusted with unlimited power."

Shakespeare adds his enlightenment: "Man, proud man! Dressed in a littlle brief authority, plays such fantastic tricks before high heaven as make the angels weep."

Let's try to make the angels smile at us. How? Never, under any circumstance, attempt running the lives of others or even suggesting that they imitate us. What then? Direct all the power we possess at self-improvement. To the extent that we devotees of freedom succeed in an understanding and explanation of our philosophy, to that extent will others be drawn to this harmonious and peaceful way of life!

26

GREATNESS

If the title of great man ought to be reserved for him who cannot be charged with an indiscretion or a vice; who spent his life in establishing the independence, the glory, and durable prosperity of his country; who succeeded in all that he undertook, and whose successes were never won at the expense of honor, justice, integrity, or by the sacrifice of a single principle—this title will not be denied to Washington.

—JARED SPARKS

A doff of the hat to George Washington, a man of pure and undeviating principle. Jared Sparks (1789–1866)—clergyman, historian, Harvard president—was a man cut from the same cloth. Washington would have been as proud of him as Sparks was of the Father of our country. Were numerous citizens in command of such righteousness as these two men exhibited, ours would be a better world. Such attainments deserve our deepest and most sincere thoughts.

Excluded from greatness are the millions who practice various forms of vice. They range, for example, from the out-and-out thief to those who use governments—federal, state and local—to do their robbing for them. A tariff, for instance, perpetrates double robbery; it robs foreigners of American customers and at the same time it robs American producers of foreign customers. It would take many more pages than space allows to list the various vices now in practice—everything from minimum wages to maximum hours to peanut subsidies.

Before emphasizing the laudable—''never the sacrifice of a single principle''—let me offer two commentaries on the destructiveness of vice.

The American clergyman Nathaniel Emmons (1745–1840):

Vice is the bane of a republic, and saps the foundations of liberty. If our industry, economy, temperance, justice and public faith are once extinguished by the opposite vices, our boasted constitution which is built on the pillars of virtue, must necessarily fall.

Edmund Burke:

Vice incapacitates a man from all public duty; it withers the power of his understanding, and makes his mind paralytic.

Napoleon was famous and feared by men for the power he wielded. While he failed to direct the lives of his wife and children, he had no doubt about his ability to direct the lives of all Frenchmen. How grateful we should be for Waterloo!

We have in the U.S.A. countless politicians and citizens who know not how to run their own lives but, like the Little Corporal, they believe in their ability to run the lives of other Americans. Reflect on the countless individuals who use all the strength they possess to gain fame, notoriety, applause, conspicuousness. Theirs is, indeed, a solitary, antisocial glory.

Let us not dwell on the results of vice but emphasize, instead, those who stand ramrod straight for justice and integrity, who would never sacrifice a single principle. These we can and should honor. The American poet William Cullen Bryant (1794–1878):

Greatness lies, not in being strong, but in the right using of strength; and strength is not used rightly when it serves only to carry a man above his fellows for his own solitary glory. He is the greatest whose strength carries up the most hearts by the attraction of his own.

Bryant, writing the above perhaps ten decades before the founding of FEE, emphasized the identical "attracting" procedure we have suggested to anyone interested in advancing the freedom philosophy: Become so proficient in understanding and explaining freedom that others will seek your tutorship. Ours is a learning and not a selling problem!

The American educator Horace Mann (1796–1859) told us that: "If any man seeks for greatness, let him forget greatness and seek for truth and he will find both."

Never seek for greatness; this is to put ambition ahead of performance. Seek first for truth and to the extent truth is discovered, to that extent will others classify one as great. Wrote the English clergyman and Dean of St. Paul's, William Ralph Inge (1860–1954): "To seek the truth, for the sake of knowing the truth, is one of the noblest objects a man can live for." The more persons who pursue this noble object, the more will freedom reign! "The truth shall make you free."

The clergyman William Ellery Channing (1780–1842):

> The greatest man is he who chooses with invincible reso-
> lution; who resists the sorest temptations from within and
> without; who bears the heaviest burdens cheerfully; who
> is calmest in storms, and most fearless under menace and
> frowns; and whose reliance on truth, on virtue, and on
> God, is most unfaltering.

Imagine, if you can, the abrupt reversal of present trends
were all clergymen to equal Channing's understanding and
example! So let us strive to emulate this great man's devo-
tion to truth, virtue and Creation!

The English statesman Lord Brougham (1778–1868), tells
us: "The true test of a great man—that, at least, which must
secure his place among the highest order of great men—is
his having been in advance of his age." Of all great men,
Jesus of Nazareth, the Perfect Exemplar, heads the list. Here
are several famous men who were in advance of their age,
listed in the order of their earthly life, and a sampling of
their pearls of wisdom.

Confucius: "Learning without thought is labor lost;
thought without learning is perilous."

Socrates: "The more I know the more I know I do not
know."

Aristotle: "Our characters are the result of our conduct."

Edmund Burke: "Depend upon it, the lovers of freedom
will be free."

Adam Smith: "Those parts of education for the teaching
of which there are no public institutions, are generally the
best taught."

John Adams: "All men are born free and equal and have certain natural, essential and unalienable rights."

Benjamin Franklin: "Where liberty dwells, there is my country."

Thomas Jefferson: "Equal rights for all, special privilege for none."

Goethe: "Epochs of faith, are epochs of fruitfulness; but epochs of unbelief, however glittering are barren of all permanent good."

Daniel Webster: "Knowledge is the only fountain, both of the love and the principles of human liberty."

Frederic Bastiat: "Where goods do not cross border lines, soldiers will."

Emerson: "Knowledge is the antidote to fear; Knowledge, Use and Reason, with its higher aids."

Grover Cleveland: "Though the people support the Government, the Government should not support the people."

Thomas Alva Edison: "Genius is one per cent inspiration and ninety-nine percent perspiration."

Calvin Coolidge: "There is no right to strike against the public safety by anybody, anywhere, anytime."

Let more of us emulate these great men, by being in advance of our age, so that freedom may reign for one and all.

NAME INDEX

118